New Places, Newfound Friends

An African Experience

John Stanton

JABIRU PUBLISHING

Published by Jabiru Publishing
PO Box 188N, Cairns North, QLD 4870, Australia
www.jabirupublishing.com.au

ISBN: 9781763863569

NATIONAL LIBRARY OF AUSTRALIA

A catalogue record for this book is available from the National Library of Australia

Cover designed by Nettie O Design, www.nettieodesign.com
Text editing and design by Wordfix, www.word-fix.com.au
Cover photograph of Deadvlei, Namibia, by John Stanton
Garamond 12.5
Printed in Australia by Kaligraphic Print,
https://kaligraphicprint.com.au

Contents

All photographs in the book were taken by the author, John Stanton.

The names of the tour company and the tour participants have been changed.

Prologue

John Stanton's life of travels and adventures spans more than four decades. Born in the Philippines to a Filipino mother and Australian father, he migrated to Australia from the Philippines with his family at the age of six months. After achieving a high school certificate, he embarked on travelling around Australia when he was 15 years old.

His life survival skills were gathering momentum despite his young age and were quickly honed. During his travels around Australia, John found work as a fruit picker, welder and brickie's labourer. He even found work in a drycleaning facility folding bed sheets. However, his life changed just six months before he was 18 years old.

"It's time to get you off the streets, young man," his father announced. Very soon after that, John found himself in Perth, Western Australia, in a chopper heading out to an offshore oil rig, thanks to his father.

This turn of events led John to a life of offshore drilling at various places around the world. His working adventures include swinging on a rope in treacherous seas between a supply vessel and a rig in the South China Sea, saving a gas platform from burning, and conducting and orchestrating countless offshore operations in the Andaman Sea, the Indian Ocean and the Gulf of Guinea off the coast of West Africa.

His life offshore has made him the calculative and methodical person he is today. However, under his hard exterior is a gentle person who has always longed for romance and that chance meeting with a soulmate.

My African Experience

Every morning or afternoon, depending on the shift I was on, a female security guard would occasionally sit with me to have a friendly chat while we ate our meals. One day I asked her what she had planned for her next week off.

"I'm going to Africa," she said with a smile.

"That sounds exciting. Whereabouts?"

"I will be spending most of my time in Ghana with friends."

As my geographical knowledge of the African continent was very poor, I had no idea where Ghana was. I had worked in Africa some years before off the coast from Gabon and Equatorial Guinea but had never thought of Africa as a holiday destination. I had my sights set on the Middle East area, including Turkey, Morocco and Egypt, for my next holiday destination. However, after some thought, and some helpful conversations with my South African friends from work, Annamarie and Dudley, I decided to research holidaying in Africa.

During my research, I came across a clip of "The Great Migration" in Africa. I decided that that was what I wanted to see. I wanted to see that migration.

I began pumping information from my South African friends at work, and they suggested a route to take and the game parks to visit. After a few weeks of researching and attempting to create an itinerary, I gave up. My travel planning skills are not very good.

Then I had the idea of looking up some African tour companies. I found an interesting company online and filled out its questionnaire, which included questions related to how long I wanted to stay, how much I wanted to spend and what I wanted to see.

After waiting for a response for nearly a week, I decided to drive to the local travel agent I had dealt with in the past. As fate would have it, the person I spoke to had been to Africa seven times and planned to continue visiting Africa.

Over the next three to four months, we would meet several times in her office to explore travel routes, flights and accommodation styles. She would suggest a draft itinerary for me to take home and review. I would return it to her several times to make changes over the course of those months.

One day in her office we found an itinerary that we both liked very much. Unfortunately, due to the time of year, I would not be able to see "The Great Migration". She said that even if

I made it to the migration area at the right time of year, it was not guaranteed that I would see the migration. I took the itinerary home for two days before taking it back to her to seal the deal!

Preparing and packing for a four-week trip to Africa with only a small bag proved to be somewhat of a challenge. The bag dimensions needed to be 80 centimetres by 35 centimetres to fit into the locker of the offroad bus. The bus, named Cynthia, was going to be my home for three and half weeks. I would be travelling with strangers, but some, I hoped, would become friends.

I packed and re-packed several times in my last week at home. As I would be travelling through four countries where the temperatures varied, this added to my frustration when packing. I bought blow-up pillows, a compact sleeping bag, and a quick-drying towel, all of which I learned later I did not need.

On 28th February 2025, I was on an afternoon Singapore Airlines flight from Cairns, Australia, to Cape Town! As the A350-900 Airbus rose above the mountains of Cairns just as the sun was setting, I looked through my business class window as the plane banked toward the east over the Coral Sea, leaving the mountains behind. A feeling of excitement filled my mind and soul.

After 13 hours in the air, a two-hour lay-over in Singapore and a one-hour layover in Johannesburg, I finally arrived in sunny

Cape Town on 1st March at 9.25 in the morning. Going through Immigration and Customs and buying a local sim card were seamless. I was met by a smiling "meet and greet" driver who gave me a welcoming handshake. We made small chit-chat along the way to the car, and then we were on the freeway to the Double Tree Hotel in Woodstock.

I spent three memorable days in Cape Town exploring Victoria Wharf, taking the cable car to Table Mountain, and visiting the local wineries.

My first morning after checking in was spent at Victoria Wharf. Thankfully, the hotel had a free shuttle bus that ran every three hours. "V & A", as it is affectionately known, is a large and exciting place. It was very busy, but I was wondering if it was because it was Saturday. There is an overwhelming number of shops, restaurants, bars and tour-booking outlets. The whole complex overlooks the bay's blue waters, with seals swimming amongst the dozens of boats cruising around, hoping for some food.

I walked around, taking in my new experience, but I was on the lookout for biltong! I found a shop that sold what I was craving for and bought a lot! However, I was not allowed to purchase Ostrich jerky if I was travelling outside South Africa.

Although it was very busy, the line-up for the Cape Town Eye was relatively quiet. I paid for a ticket and had a bird's eye view of the complex, the water, boats of every description, and Table Mountain in the background. It was breathtaking. After disembarking from the Cape Town Eye, I walked to the shuttle bus pick-up point and waited for the shuttle bus to take me back to the hotel.

Victoria Wharf in Cape Town

That afternoon I was back at the hotel enjoying a cold Windhoek lager and one of the best cooked rump steaks I had had in a long time. The steak was not just a standard 25-

millimetre cut of rump. It was almost thick enough to be a roast, and it was cooked perfectly.

The next morning, I enquired at Reception as to how to travel to Table Mountain.

"Sir, we can arrange a taxi for you with a reputable taxi company that will take you to the ticket purchasing point at the bottom of the mountain."

"That sounds perfect."

The woman picked up the phone and made a booking with the taxi company.

"Your taxi is on its way, sir. Please walk to the front of the hotel where you will be met and taken to Table Mountain."

The driver was quite chatty along the way. When we arrived, he explained that this was the pick-up point for after I returned from the top of the mountain.

"All you have to do is call us when you are on your way down, and one of us will meet you here."

I thanked and paid him and walked toward the long queue at the ticketing booth. I stood in line for more than an hour, and it was getting hot as there was not much shade. As I moved closer to the ticketing window, I overheard the person in front of me say, "Why do I need to give you my phone number?"

"We need a phone number for safety reasons, sir," was the reply from the ticketing person. I was so glad that I had made a handwritten note of my local South African phone number when I purchased my sim card.

It was then my turn to stand in front of the ticketing window.

"May I have your phone number, sir?"

I gave him my number like I was a local! He presented me with my boarding ticket for the cable car and pointed in the direction I should walk to join the boarding queue. I waited in this queue for another hour before I boarded the cable car. We were then squashed into the cable car, shoulder to shoulder. Even though we were so close together, the floor on the cable car revolved as it travelled, enabling everyone to take good photos.

Table Mountain, Cape Town

The six-minute ride to the top was breathtaking. After disembarking the cable car at the top, I found coffee shops, souvenir shops, a restaurant and bar, and dozens of walking trails. The stone walking trails were well-worn from use by thousands of tourists every year. Apparently, I was lucky to be there on a sunny day. There was not a cloud in the sky, and I must have taken dozens of photos and videos.

View of Cape Town from Table Mountain

I had a video conversation with my son Tom from up there and showed him around as I was walking. I bought several souvenirs, as one does, and stopped for a coffee. One souvenir I bought was a nice notebook for myself. The cover was made of cork, and I thought it was quite unique. It became my best friend for the next four weeks, as I wrote in it every day on my tour of Africa.

After a few hours of walking and gazing at the coastline and cliff structures, it was time to go. As I was descending in the cable car, I called the taxi company to meet me and take me back to my hotel.

I quickly went to my room to pick up some more Nicorette and drop off my souvenirs. The driver kindly waited for me and then took me to V & A where I stayed for lunch and some beers overlooking the water. It is a fantastic place. I had squid calamari, but it was not cut into rings like normal. These were whole baby squids with chips and salad.

After lunch I did a little bar hopping and window shopping and stopped to watch a group of people singing under a tree. They were great dancers and had excellent singing voices.

I found the hotel shuttle bus in the same place as the day before and went back to the hotel to chill out after a big day. I rang Reception and organised for a car and driver to take me around the wineries the next day. I thought about hiring a car but remembered that if I was going to be wine tasting I did not want to be pulled over and spend the rest of my holiday in an African gaol. Not that I think it would have come to that but why take the chance? Also, I had no idea where to go!

After another great breakfast I met with my driver for the day. He was a nice guy and very informative. We explored the Stellenbosch area, which is very scenic. We were at the first winery around 10.00 am, and people were in there drinking already! It was too early for me, and so I just walked around the grounds. At the entrance to the restaurant there were three stones. When you held your hands about 100 millimetres from the stones and moved your hands up and down, the stones made a sound. Apparently, they pick up on your energies. I thought it was a bit of a gimmick and was looking around for a power cord or a speaker, but there were no electronics anywhere.

The next winery had an animal enclosure out the back. They had lions, normal tigers and a white tiger. I think the white tiger was imported. It was still too early for a drink! I cannot remember the names of the first two wineries, but the next one was called Glen Carlou. Friends of my eldest son Jack in Cambodia know the people who own it and recommended I go there.

Now it was time for a drink! I sampled some whites and reds along with a platter of cheeses. The woman speaking to me about the wines was young and very informative. I wondered how she had obtained so much knowledge at a young age. She said wine was her favourite drink. I did not buy any wine, but just sipped on wine and ate cheese while gazing at the many acres of grape vines from the elevated view.

One of the wineries near Cape Town

Our next place was called Graff winery. This one was a bit classier than the others, with an expensive clothes shop and an art gallery. I was greeted at the entrance by a beautiful woman who explained the layout of the building, the bar and shop locations, and the direction in which to find clothing and artworks.

This place overlooked the mountains whereas the last place overlooked the fields. I was shown to a table where I waited for service. A waiter finally arrived and presented me with the wine tastings. His talk about the different wines in the region was not as pleasant or enthusiastic as the woman in the Glen Carlou winery. I found him a little bit rude.

I had smoked salmon and cheese with my wine this time and could not wait to leave due to the rudeness of the waiter. I paid my bill and walked to the carpark where I found my trusty driver waiting for me. He waved at me with a beaming smile.

"How was it, sir?"

"Really good. I enjoyed it." I did not mention the waiter.

It was a pleasant drive back to the hotel, with enjoyable conversations with the driver. When we arrived, I felt that I needed to tip him more than the average tip.

After another full day, it was time to unwind at the hotel bar. That afternoon I had a planned meeting with the tour operator for pre-departure formalities. I seated myself in the Reception area with my drink, waiting. I had no idea what he or she looked like. Soon other people began sitting in chairs around me, and I assumed they were part of the tour. When a person with a beaming smile wearing a bucket hat and holding a folder entered the Reception area, I knew that he was our guide.

He introduced himself as Anesu from Roaming Safaris. He spoke to us about the forms we needed to complete then so that we did not have to wait in the morning. Along with other people, I filled out the necessary paperwork and made small chit-chat with the strangers who would become my travelling companions for the next three and a half weeks. Not all of them were there, and I was to meet the rest of them in the morning.

I checked out in the morning and carried my bag to the front of the hotel, to find a bus called Cynthia with Roaming Safaris stickers on the front.

I was the first to arrive, and I recognised Anesu. We shook hands and greeted each other, and then sat on a low brick retaining wall talking about the trip as other people started to arrive. I think it was Leon and Matteo first, and then Martina joined shortly after. The four of us stowed our bags in the bus lockers and locked the doors with our padlocks. We returned to the retaining wall, sitting and waiting for the other passengers to arrive while getting to know about each other's country of origin. Eventually everyone arrived and stowed their bags. We had the usual greeting.

"Hi, where are you from?"

After the rest of the bags were stowed in the bus lockers, we left Cape Town at 8.20 am on an adventure that would take us to Namibia, Botswana and Zimbabwe. As we left Cape Town I felt really excited. This is a rarity for me! We stopped at the top of Table Mountain nature park for one last look down at Cape Town. We made use of the mobile coffee vans there and had an extra coffee. After exploring and taking photos, the twelve of us reboarded the bus and drove to a mall in a suburb called Tableview. Anesu needed to purchase food supplies, and we were there for about an hour. I bought beer and biltong supplies and had another coffee. I wondered why Anesu had not shopped for supplies the previous day instead of making us wait in a mall while on our tour.

We travelled on a bitumen highway to the next place for a toilet stop at Winkelshoek Padstal. A few of us bought more biltong and droewors. After a group photo in front of Cynthia, we hit the road again for a few more hours before stopping at a lay-by to make lunch. The landscape was changing, becoming more mountainous and rockier. This was one of many lunches and dinners we would eat sitting in camping chairs outside the bus. Everyone helped prepare the food, which consisted of salami, ham and salad with bread rolls.

During lunch, I struck up a conversation with Martina from Spain, and Kondjeni (the bus driver) from Namibia. Anesu was from Zimbabwe. Martina and I seemed to get along straight away, despite a big language barrier. Her English was a bit hard to understand, and I knew very few words in Spanish.

After lunch we all helped pack things away. After a few more hours on the road we arrived at our accommodation, the Marcrusaal Campground in Cederberg. The group was divided into "accommodated" and "tented" guests. It was a personal preference before booking the tour whether we wanted to stay in a room or put up a tent every day. I opted to be in a room every night. I think there were seven people staying in tents. They had the option to upgrade for a price if they wanted, whenever we reached the accommodation places. As the days went on, I think three of them upgraded to rooms when they could.

The travelling time that day was seven hours and 25 minutes over just 200 kilometres. Not all that time was spent driving, however. It was a nice drive into the campground, away from the highway. There were many citrus trees on the property.

Once we stopped and unloaded everything, everyone got busy either moving into their rooms or putting up tents. My room was quite nice with air-conditioning, TV and a fridge. I would say it was worth three stars. I unpacked and prepared my clothes for the next day as I knew we would have an early start.

My travel agent had suggested that I bring a sleeping bag as some of the lodges sometimes forget to change the sheets. This sleeping bag travelled with me for four weeks, and it was never used!

The lodge had a pool where some of us met after settling in. Some people jumped in, but I did not like the look of the water and stayed out of it. I went back to my room, grabbed a beer, and walked to the camp kitchen. I found Kondjeni chilling on the stairs looking at his phone. He looked up at me.

"Why are you not swimming, Mr John?"

"I don't like the colour of the water, mate." We both had a little chuckle, just as Martina joined us. In her thick Spanish accent, she asked if she could have one of my beers.

"Of course," I said. I walked back to my room, which was next door to the camp kitchen, to retrieve one from the fridge. We talked over a couple of beers, but then it was getting close to dinner time at the lodge. We left our tranquil session and dispersed to change and get ready for dinner. We did not have to cook that night.

When we arrived at the restaurant in the main lodge, there was a long table nicely prepared for us. After we had all arrived and were seated, the manager spoke to us about the area and the fruit farm, and the history of the farm. After the talk, she invited us to walk toward the two women standing behind a table with pots of food.

We lined up behind each other in front of the two women, and we were served chicken stew that had lots of little bones in it. Martina, who was sitting next to me, kept giving a dog the chicken bones. I guess the dog was part of the lodge.

After dinner, Anesu gave us a talk about the plan for the following day's trip. Soon after, most of the group walked back to their respective accommodation. I stayed with Martina and Leon (from Austria) for a few more wines and then called it a night.

Anesu cooked scrambled eggs in the morning for those who wanted it, but there were fruit and cereal as well. Breakfast set us up for the big day ahead.

We left the Marcrusaal lodge at 7.40 am. The bitumen road to our next accommodation on the Orange River was good, with very few potholes, but it was a long day. The landscape was continuously changing: vast hills, and rocky and sandy terrain. We made two "bushy-bushy" (pee stops) before pulling up to make lunch at about 1.00 pm. This roadside stop was a bit messy: broken bottles, some rubbish and – worst of all – human faeces. I would not have seen the faeces if I had not gone for a walk away from everyone for a pee. Not all the roadside stops were like that one. Some of them were quite nice.

After lunch we made one more stop in Springbok for alcohol supplies before crossing over the Namibian border. Passport control took a very long time, even though we had filled in our immigration forms while we were in Springbok. There was only one passport controller on duty at that time.

Border crossing between South Africa and Namibia

Namibia

Not long after crossing the border we saw a giraffe on the side of the road. This was a big moment for me. I became very emotional! I could not believe what I was looking at and what I was feeling! I mean, holy shit! What was happening to me? I rarely get emotional but seeing this majestic animal in the wild did something to me. I still get emotional even now, thinking about it and looking at the photo I took. I cannot remember if it was a male or a female, but it was huge: big body, and very long neck. I kept staring at it, taking in all the features of this majestic, beautiful giraffe. It was literally staring at me staring at it. Well, it was probably staring at all of us on the bus, but I like to think it was staring at me.

Giraffes have a hard life. They have very little sleep as they sleep standing up for short periods at a time, because they are not able to lie down. Even when drinking water, they need to spread their front legs as wide as possible to allow their long necks to lower down to drink. Even then, they are not able to keep their heads down for very long as all the blood would rush to their heads.

The first giraffe I saw on my trip

We arrived at our next accommodation, the Felix Unite Lodge on the Orange River at 5.30 pm. It had been a long day: almost ten hours to cover more than over 500 kilometres. The drive into the lodge was very picturesque, with the grounds just 100 metres from the river.

Felix Unite Lodge on the Orange River

We pulled up at the camping ground which was up higher than the cabins. The accommodated people had to carry their bags down to the cabins as the bus could not drive down there. It was about a 150-metre walk. Some of the older ones found it a bit exhausting.

In the group there were five of us who had booked rooms for the whole trip, while seven of the group had chosen to stay in tents. During the trip some of the campers would upgrade to rooms, as setting up and pulling down tents every day was getting a bit onerous. Also, they were rained out a couple of times.

My cabin overlooking the river was rustic and comfortable. There was no fridge or TV, and this was something I would get used to during the trip.

The pool bar at Felix Unite Lodge

Once everyone was settled, some of us met and had drinks at the pool. As I was still not "in tune" with some people, I just had a quick dip and walked up to the bar which was only 20 metres away. Matteo (from Switzerland) and Kondjeni joined me. Of all the people on the trip, I was most in tune with Matteo, Kondjeni, Anesu, Martina, Ella and Mila (sisters from Germany), Liam from Ireland and Leon.

The people I never seemed to get in tune with were two couples from New Zealand. They were older and a bit "upper class", and all worked in highly paid professional positions. Although I was never able to get in tune with them, we would converse a little – when they would allow us to talk and not talk over the top of us.

We rounded off the afternoon with an early barbeque. Brad helped with the cooking that night, which was a sort of Cumbrian sausage on the grill. After all the clearing-up was completed, Matteo and I walked down to the pool bar and enjoyed each other's company until the bar closed at 10.00 pm.

The next day was to be a relatively short day compared with the trip the previous day. Breakfast was not until 8.00 am. Kondjeni found a way to drive the bus down to the cabins where we loaded the rest of the baggage.

We left the lodge at 9.00 am, stopping a short distance up the road to refuel. However, the network was down, and Anesu had no way to pay for the fuel. He had a bit of cash but not enough to fill up the bus. So, I suggested to the group that they might like to help pay for the fuel. Some people volunteered, and some had selective hearing. I put in 1300 rand, Ella and Mila put in a few hundred rand, and Matteo put in 400 rand. It was our first obstacle of the trip, but we overcame it.

This was the first time that we encountered gravel roads. Although the road was good, the dust from the oncoming vehicles would enter the bus as our windows were open due to the lack of air conditioning. This was fine, and no one seemed to complain about it.

When we left the gravel road and came onto the bitumen, we pulled over for a group photo. Also, Anesu talked to us about some of the plant life around the area.

We continued our journey, and I was surprised when we drove into a small town that Anesu told us we were close to a winery. The small shacks that lined the side of the road were the housing for the winery workers. It is very desolate in this area, and a winery was the last thing I expected to see. The small town had a few small shops and an ATM. Anesu took some money out from the ATM and repaid us for the fuel money we gave him earlier.

Lunch was at a place called Fish River Canyon. A permit needed to be obtained before driving in. As this took about 20 minutes to obtain, some of us went to the nearby shop. I came across a map of Namibia, which was to be one of my best souvenirs as I marked the roads we took along the way.

Once we were allowed in, Kondjeni drove us to a viewing point where we could see the massive canyon that stretched on, seemingly forever. He dropped us there while he and Anesu drove to an elevated shaded lookout and information centre.

As I walked along the edge of the canyon, all I could say was, "Fuckin' wow!" It was absolutely breathtaking. The mind boggles as to how this formation was created. Part of me realises that it was made by nature, but most of me thinks that perhaps another "being" was mining here, and this was the result of their mining efforts. Nonetheless, the whole experience was breathtaking, and worth another visit one day. We walked along the rim of the canyon to the lookout where Anesu and Kondjeni were waiting for us. It was about 1.5 kilometres away, and the weather was very hot!

Fish River Canyon

Lunch consisted of pasta salad. We sat at tables and ate while gazing at the magnificent views. Matteo helped with the preparing and cooking, and we all helped with the clearing up. We were all eager to help at this stage of the trip, but toward the end of the trip there would be fewer people wanting to help – me included – but the younger ones were always keen.

We continued our trip to Keetmanshoop, with stops along the way to take photos of animals on the side of the road: zebras, giraffes, springboks and baboons. Some photos turned out well, but for most photos the animals were too far away. Thankfully, Leon is a photographer. Using all his lenses, he managed to capture some good long-distance shots. We had a group chat on WhatsApp where some people would upload their photos. I was glad that Leon knew how to upload to WhatsApp.

It was hard to believe that these animals were just roaming free on the sides of the roads. It was such a fantastic thing to see.

We reached our accommodation, the Schutzenhaus Lodge in Keetmanshoop after travelling for six hours and 45 minutes over 300 kilometres. It was an overcast afternoon, but still hot enough for a cold beer by the pool. My room was very modern with all the usual comforts – air conditioning, fridge, big bathroom – but what I found during the whole trip was that most rooms did not have a power point next to the bed. So, I had to charge my phone away from my bed on a desk. This was a bit worrying as I needed my alarm for the early starts each morning. I also learned that all the rooms had two types of plugs: a two-pin plug and a three-pin plug. I assumed the three-pin type was the older style. I had bought a plug in Cairns before I left, but even though the packaging said it was suitable for South Africa, there was no way it was going to fit in any of the sockets there. I ended up buying a three-pin plug from a souvenir shop in Etosha.

Bar at Keetwanshoop

There is a very big German influence in Keetmanshoop. In fact, there is a big German influence all over this part of Africa. Everybody at the bar in the lodge spoke German. They were even playing some sort of German bar game. Everywhere in the bar had flags of different German towns and soccer teams. Big stein mugs were on display on shelves throughout the bar.

We had an included dinner which was chicken schnitzel! Very German.

After dinner, Anesu gave us his usual after-dinner speech about what to expect on the next day. Just as he was about to elaborate, Brad spoke above him in a loud voice to Carol, saying that some president in another country had just died. He was reading the news while Anesu was talking. I thought that was very rude!

After dinner, Matteo and I went to the bar, where Leon and Martina joined us. It was a good night, and we ended up leaving the bar at about 11.00.

It was a clunky start the next morning for our trip to the Namib-Naukluft National Park. Our alarms were set at 5.00 am for a 6.00 am start, but at 5:30 am, Anesu made a group call to all of us, saying that it was raining and we would be delayed. I went back to sleep, but then the phone rang again. This time it was Liam who in his thick Irish accent said, "Is anyone getting up?"

Poor fella, I don't think he got the first call from Anesu at 5:30 am. He was at the bus wondering where everyone was.

We eventually left Keetmanshoop at 7.30 am and stopped at the Giants Playground. It is an area covered with natural rock boulders that have been individually split in straight lines and stacked on top of each other. Anesu informed us that it is called the Giants Playground because of an old wives tale that giants used to throw rocks at each other. However, the scientific reason is that high temperature and erosion caused the rocks to appear as they are today. It would be very easy to get lost here.

Giants' Playground

When we knew that nobody was lost in the playground and everyone was accounted for, our journey continued to the

Quiver Tree Forest, which is very close to the Giants' Playground. We went for a walk through the stark forest, led by Anesu who knew everything about the trees and the animals that live in this forest. It was not a forest in the usual sense. This forest was quite barren, but alive with natural-living and self-protecting species, including plants, trees and mammals.

After a short visit to the forest, we continued our journey to Mariental. The rain seemed to be gathering everywhere around us as we stopped for food supplies. We travelled via a long bitumen road from the forest to Mariental, and ear pods were our best friends on roads like this. Some people slept, some read, some played games on their phones. Thankfully, the bus had USB ports in every seat.

While Anesu was food shopping, the rest of us were walking around the shops when suddenly there was the loudest sound like a gunshot. I literally thought I was standing next to someone with a gun. It turned out it was a massive crack of thunder. There was no lead-up to it, no rumbling, and not even any dark clouds. Suddenly, the rain just poured down, and the locals were so happy that some were even dancing. Apparently, they do not get much rain in this area.

The car park suddenly flooded, and the streets turned into rivers. I was trapped at the entrance to the toilets with Martina and Carol, waiting for the rain to slow down, but we were still getting wet, and the rain was not likely to slow down soon. I decided to make a run for it into the arcade where I waited until the rain stopped. Then, some of us decided to wade through the flooded carpark back to the bus to wait for everyone else.

It was a short but intense downpour. We saw cars drive through the flooded streets while waiting for Anesu to return. It was amazing to watch the flooded streets slowly return to normal before our eyes.

Anesu arrived with a shopping trolley full of food. Some of us helped store it either in the fridge or in the bus compartments. Martina would always be the first to help with whatever needed to be done, and she promptly started storing the food under Anesu's instructions. Some of us helped as well, but some would stand around chatting. I guess if all twelve of us helped we would get in each other's way. Some local kids hung around hoping for some food, but we could not give them any. So some of us gave them small amounts of cash instead.

Once everything was stored away, we continued on our way and drove through a storm which might have been the same one that hit us while we were shopping. After we passed the storm, we drove on a bit further and found a place to stop and cook some lunch, which consisted of burgers, salad and cooked onions. That was the thing about the whole trip: we did not really have any authentic African food. Anesu cooked us a variety of stews and curries that were his own recipes. One time, he introduced us to eating with our hands using polenta instead of the Indian way of using chapati bread.

As we cooked, the weather changed to squally conditions, and the sky turned black in the distance. The storm was coming closer. We had to hurry up and eat and not worry about washing the dishes. We would wash them when we arrived at our next accommodation. Obviously, we had not put enough distance between us and the storm.

The storm approaching the bus

We arrived at Hammerstein Lodge in the Namib-Naukluft National Park where we would stay for two nights, allowing us time to wash some clothes. We arrived at 5.15 pm, making it nearly a 10-hour day over 400 kilometres. There was evidence that the lodge had recently been hit by a storm. As the camping site was flooded, four of the campers managed to up-grade to rooms. Martina stayed at the camp site in her tent. I think she always stayed in her tent wherever we stopped, except for a couple of times when rooms were included, because the campers were required to stay in rooms for safety reasons.

The power was out, and the wi-fi was down. I walked to my room to drop off my bag, only to find a puddle of water on the floor. It did not seem to be coming from a leaking roof. There was no dripping from the ceiling, just a puddle on the floor. I enquired at Reception, and the staff promptly cleaned up the puddle for me.

There was nothing left to do but go to the bar. I did not feel like going in the pool as there was still a bit of thunder and lightning around. The beer was still cold, despite the power blackout.

I sat down on a leather chair in the lounge, and started updating my diary until Brad joined me, and then Matteo. As Brad had travelled extensively with his wife Carol, I asked him about the Middle East as that was where I wanted to travel the following year: Turkey, Egypt and Morocco. We spoke about it for a while, and he was quite informative. The wi-fi came back on, and that was the end of that conversation!

We all met at the camping site for dinner at 7.30 pm. The meal consisted of a chicken curry that Anesu and Matteo had cooked. I brought over a beer for Matteo and Anesu and a wine for myself. It had just started to drizzle but the rain did not get any heavier. As usual, we all had an enjoyable meal and listened to Anesu's talk about the next day's adventure.

Most of the people had left, leaving just Matteo, Martina, Anesu, Kondjeni and me sitting around talking and finishing up our drinks. I decided to get my map of Namibia out and mark the roads we had taken and the roads we were about to take for the rest of the tour, with the help of Anesu. Looking at the route we would take in the upcoming days indicated that we were going to be very close to the Angolan border.

After exploring the map and completing the final clearing up of dishes and food, we said goodnight. I went to the bar for one more wine and then brought one back to my room. When I entered, I found that the puddle on the floor had returned and there was now a distinct leak coming from the ceiling. As I could not do anything about it, I just walked around the puddle to enter the bathroom so I could have a shower. After that, I turned off the lights and went to sleep.

The next morning was nice, dry and sunny. We prepared for our day trip with home-made pancakes and fruit.

This part of Namibia is sand dune country, and even to this day when I think back, I find myself daydreaming about missing it. Our plan was to drive to a famous sand dune called Dune 45, where we would walk along the ridge to the top.

Along the way we crossed a few small creeks that were flowing but still passable. We stopped at the Tsauchab River which was too deep and running too fast as a result of the storms the day before. There were about 15 vehicles parked on the side of the road waiting for the river to go down. Anesu made the decision to turn back and drive to a different sand dune which we could walk up. He said that this sand dune is nearly identical to Dune 45. The only difference is that Dune 45 is about 170 metres high whereas this one is about 250 metres. The only other difference is that this dune does not have a name.

We arrived at the base of the dune, and as I looked up at the dune I said to myself, "This is going to be easy." I had to eat my words when I started to climb along the ridge. I have never experienced anything like it. The sand gave way as I walked on it, making it a "one step forward, two steps back" scenario. My calves started burning, and I had to stop to rest every ten minutes. Even resting did not relieve the burning as I was still standing at the angle where my calves were over-stretched. I soon worked out that every time I stopped, I would have to turn around to face down the dune to reverse the over-stretching of my calves. Even the two German girls, Mila and Ella, who play tennis and are very fit, could not make it to the top. Martina and Matteo were way ahead of all of us and walked straight to the top, only stopping to take photos.

To walk up a dune you need balance. This is hard to achieve as most of your concentration is focused on how to relieve the burning sensation in your calves. You cannot just walk straight up the face of it. We had to walk along the gradually inclining ridge, which was only about 500 millimetres wide and not very compacted, and we had to take small steps instead of normal strides. I found it easier to walk in other people's footprints as the sand was a bit more compacted there, allowing greater traction.

The dune with no name

I took so many photos, videos and creative photography on my Samsung phone. If I have one regret about this trip it is that I should have bought a good camera like several people had suggested.

It is very hard to describe in words how this land looks and feels. It is one thing to marvel at the landscape on the ground, but when you are up high and panning around, there is a different dynamic. As I looked around at the land below me, and at the dune around me, I found myself getting emotional and talking to myself, saying, "Holy shit! Holy shit!" several times: the vastness, the colours, the perfect contrast of flowing rivers amongst desolate sand and rocky outcrops. Put simply, it was breathtakingly and absolutely beautiful. There are not enough words in the English dictionary to describe what I was seeing.

It was time to turn back and walk down. I did not quite make it to the top due to exhaustion, but the level I made it to was enough for me. Most of the group turned around at the same point.

While we were recovering in the shade of the bus, we looked down in the distance toward the swollen river crossing. We noticed that some vehicles were managing to cross the river that had been too deep to cross earlier. Anesu decided we would drive to the river to see if it was safe for Cynthia to cross once everyone came back from their dune climb.

When we arrived at the river, there were smaller vehicles still waiting for the river to subside. Kondjeni and Anesu decided that the river had subsided enough and that it was safe for our vehicle to cross. We crossed it with ease, and I took a great video of the event. When we were on the other side we headed for the salt and clay pans of Sossusvlei, passing Dune 45 on the way.

Dead trees at Deadvlei

We had to park the bus at a rendezvous point where we were met by an open-sided 4 x 4 vehicle and a 4 x 4 SUV which took us all to the start of a walking trail that led to Deadvlei. The history of Deadvlei is that around 900 years ago the area dried up and the dunes formed, cutting it off from the river and making it too dry for the trees to survive. They died where they stood, turning black from the sun. In a way, they are still beautiful and make for some great creative photography. It was about an hour's return walk. I was again in awe of the surrounding sand dunes. I took dozens of photos and videos of this area, but they cannot do the place justice. At this point, I decided that I needed to come back again.

The walk itself was very easy compared with walking along the ridge of a sand dune. Once arriving at the dried-up lake with its impressive dead trees, I was once again in awe of my surroundings. It was a peaceful, beautiful arid land.

Our 4 x 4 SUVs transferred us back to the bus where Kondjeni was waiting for us. Once we were all on board, we drove to a place called Sesriem campground where we made use of the bar and restaurant. Anesu had booked a table which was prepared before our arrival. Lunch was included on the day trip, but we were only allowed to order burgers and soft drinks. Alcohol was at our own expense.

After lunch, we drove back to Hammerstein lodge via the Sesriem canyon. I did not really get much from it, and I doubt that anyone else did either, except for some of the girls who took the opportunity to go for a pee. Once we were back at the lodge, it was time for a rest and some beers before a barbeque dinner.

I noticed a girl working at the bar who was there the day before. Her name was Christina, and she had the most beautiful smile. We chatted for a while in between her serving drinks to other customers.

The next morning as I walked to the bus preparing to depart, Christina ran up to me in the courtyard, with a beaming smile on her face.

"Good morning, John."

"Good morning, Christina."

"I wish you weren't leaving today."

I spoke to her about my feelings about the Namibian desert and said, "I'm sure I'll be back some day, Christina. I love this place."

She handed me a piece of paper with her phone number written on it.

"This is so you can call me and tell me about Australia."

I had never had that happen to me before. Christina and I still chat on WhatsApp now and again. At first, she was messaging me every day, and sometimes several times a day. She called me later when I was in Swakopmund, and I learned that she was only 27 years old. She looked older than that. We only message each other every other day now.

Our trip from Hammerstein lodge to Bushman's Desert Camp was an easy four hours and 30 minutes' drive over 165 kilometres. It was quite a desolate and rough drive, with not much to look at. Even the sand dunes changed colour to a shade of beige; no more burnt-orange colours. There were still a few animals, like springboks and ostriches, worth stopping for.

We also stopped to take more group photos, and for bushy bushy.

We stopped at a small place called Solitaire. There were only a couple of cafés, a motel and fuel. For some reason there were a few old cars rusting away. Martina and I got inside one and had our photo taken by Carol. We all had coffee and snacks and bought some souvenirs.

We arrived at the Bushman's Desert Camp after driving down what seemed like the entrance to a canyon. We found the camp at the bottom of the track. The campground was on the right as we drove down, and on the left was a bar that sold non-perishable foods and souvenirs. Further on were the cabins. Kondjeni dropped us closer to the cabins, so that we had only a short distance to carry our bags. The door keys were in the lock, and once I let myself into the cabin, I thought to myself, "What the hell have I walked into here?" No air conditioning, no wi-fi, and it was a cash-only bar and shop. And it was hot! But the ambience made up for it, and as I became used to the environment and lack of "mod-cons", it became an awesome place.

After unpacking and settling in, I walked up to the camping area where Anesu and Matteo were cooking lunch in the covered camp kitchen area. Lunch was a mixture of beans and vegetables with pasta.

After lunch, Anesu announced that we would be going on an open-sided safari at 2.00 pm and that we should all meet at 1:45 at the bar. This gave some of us time to either take a nap or to explore.

We all met at the bar at 1.45 where we were introduced to Francis, who was the manager of the desert camp. We boarded the vehicle, along with Anesu who decided to join us for the tour around the desert.

Guest rooms at Bushman's Camp

We saw plenty of springboks and ostriches. It was an astonishingly beautiful place, full of contrasting mountains and sand dunes. Our guide would stop and give us a talk about the animals, spiders and snakes in the area. It was very interesting to learn that the deadliest spider would not purposely harm a human as our footsteps were too heavy.

We drove along the fence line and learned that many ostriches either get killed or are left to die on the fence. They do not know how to jump over it and get caught in the wire.

After returning from the tour, some people went to their rooms, and some hung around the bus and chatted. I rested near the bar, writing in my diary and gazing at the beautiful desert dunes.

The dunes seen from Bushman's Camp

As I was gazing around in between writing sentences, I noticed Martina sitting on a rock, less than one hundred metres away. She appeared to be meditating. After a while she walked toward me and sat down. I sensed there was something wrong.

"Are you OK?" She looked at me with tears in her eyes.

"No."

A few days before, she had told me that she and her father had planned to come on this trip together, but he had passed away about three years before. I knew she had been thinking about him while sitting on that rock looking at the moon rising over the dunes. I held her hand to console her, and we sat and talked a little about her home in Spain and about her father. Sometimes we just sat quietly, listening to the silence of the desert. It may not be possible to understand the silence of the desert unless you have been there and experienced it – in Africa.

After the tour ended, I met Martina in Johannesburg for dinner. We talked about that evening in the desert. We had a connection with each other and also shared a connection with the desert. Maybe she meant it when she said that we would meet again in the same place.

We both stood to get ready for dinner by the bus. We had a big, long hug, and Martina said, "Thank you."

Matteo had prepared and cooked shepherd's pie and vegetables for dinner. He is a good cook and cooks a lot at home. After everyone had helped clean up, I walked back to the bar and bought some beer and wine for Anesu and Matteo. It was a warm night, but we managed to find firewood and light a fire. We sat around listening to Anesu's stories about African customs and food, and his childhood. Everyone was very interested in African customs.

Some of the others said good night and started to walk back to their rooms. There were only Anesu, Matteo, Martina, Kondjeni and I left. I felt like being alone. So I said goodnight, stopping by the bar for a wine to take back to my room.

Once in my room, I remembered that Francis told us that the animals do not come near the cabins. So, when I reached my room, I opened all the sliding doors to the veranda. I could not believe what I was experiencing. I think I can say that this room was the best room I have ever stayed in. The veranda was only about a metre above the ground and about four metres wide. It had a brick barbeque and outdoor sink, and table and chairs.

I sat there on the veranda for a good hour with an almost full moon, looking at the dunes and just listening to the silence. I have no words that could even remotely explain my emotions at that time.

We watched the morning sun come up from the camp kitchen while Anesu cooked us eggs, beans and sausages. Leon had been up early to set up his tripod, camera and lenses. Martina was down at the bottom of the hill 50 metres away while Leon took some creative photography of Martina's silhouette in the rising sunlight coming over the dunes. Everybody was snapping away from different places to get that perfect shot of the sunrise. I climbed up to the top of the hill and filmed the sunrise in hyper-lapse speed. It turned out all right, but it was not a great video.

The sun was up now, and we started eating breakfast and talking about the spectacular sunrise. We all helped with the dishwashing and packing up. Once we were on the bus, we drove down to our cabins to pick up our bags. We left the Bushman's camp at 7.30 am. As I looked back, I wished I could have stayed longer.

For about two and a half hours I was still in awe of the desert until we stopped at the Tropic of Capricorn sign for several group photos. We were about to say goodbye to the desert as we continued our journey to the coastal town of Walvis Bay.

Tropic of Capricorn sign

The land was continually changing from the burnt-orange dunes to light-beige rock and mountains. We left the gravel road and turned north on the welcoming bitumen highway. Our speed increased to 120 kilometres an hour, and a sense of anticipation came over us.

As our route came closer to the coast, the dunes had returned but were now pale-beige, low, windswept and longer in length. When the ocean appeared it was an interesting sight to see the sand dunes on one side of the highway and the ocean on the other. Palm trees lined the highway as we approached the city, reminding me of Dubai.

Beige sand dunes on the way to Walvis Bay

We arrived in Walvis Bay and spent about an hour in a shopping mall for more supplies and some decent coffee. We lost Liam for a while, but he eventually made it back to the bus. By then, it was lunch time. So we drove to the esplanade, found a place to park close to the water and set up. Lunch consisted of hotdogs. This particular spot is famous for pink flamingos. Unfortunately, they were too far away to take good photos of them.

A woman in her car parked close to us said something to us in German. Thankfully, we had four German-speaking people with us. Apparently, she was trying to sell us some home-made pickled mussels. We were a bit dubious about them, and we all declined.

During the pack-up we encountered some trouble sliding the tables under the bus. The slide had been damaged during the corrugations on the gravel road, and it would be a challenge each time we needed to pack them away. After some perseverance we managed to slide the tables in place and secure them. It was then a short 40-minute drive to Swakopmund.

During the short coastal drive, it was interesting to see a couple of oil rigs out on the water – a jack-up drilling rig and a semi-submersible. There were also groups of beach-casting fishermen. As we crossed the bridge into Swakopmund, we saw our first herd of camels along the dried-up river. That was a surprise!

Just past the bridge was the booking centre where we could book individual activities for our free day in the morning. We were presented with a short video of all the activities available. Ella, Mila, Martina, and I chose the dolphin and seal cruise, Liam booked the sand-boarding activity, Leon and Matteo did not book anything and the four professional people (Carol, Brad, Steve and Sue) tried to get on a scenic flight but it was too expensive. Theresa and Brad booked a couple of push bikes instead, and I think Steve and Sue did not book anything.

Before we left the booking centre, we discussed restaurants and decided on a seafood restaurant called 1905 for the evening meal. We left the booking centre for the short drive to our accommodation, the Haus Garnison. The trip from Bushman's Camp took seven hours, and we arrived at 2.30 pm.

Everyone retrieved their luggage from the bus. This took quite a while because some of the professional people did not listen to instructions, and the guest house manager had to patiently wait for them.

After we had a briefing from the guest house manager, I carried my bag and settled into my room to chill out for a while. My room was a very nice and bright room with all the mod-cons. I decided to go for a walk. My swollen big toe, which was not getting any better, proved to be a slight hindrance.

It was not an overly nice-looking part of town, but a few blocks away I managed to find the beach, which was very nice. I limped along for a while and found a cove with a few bars and restaurants. I stopped at the closest bar and ordered a Windhoek Lager. I was enjoying the sunshine and the beach when a group of singers arrived and started singing and dancing in front of us. Of course, I had to take a video and send it to my South African friend Dudley from Darwin. He replied that it was a typical dance for tourists. That did not worry me as I did not know what an authentic dance was. No sooner had I sent the video than one of the dancers started walking amongst us asking for donations and trying to sell their CDs. Dudley was right!

I left the bar and limped back to the guest house to get ready for Kondjeni and Anesu to pick us up with the bus for our evening at the seafood restaurant. Apparently, it was about a ten-minute drive.

I expected it to be a typical indoors restaurant, but when we parked the bus in a carpark in front of the ocean looking at a jetty, I started to wonder. It was a bit cool and windy, and I was glad I had brought along the jacket which I had thrown in my bag before I left Australia as a "just in case" item.

Pier 1905

We all disembarked the bus to embrace the windy conditions. Anesu led us to an old wooden staircase that ascended to the jetty. Once we were on the jetty the wind was even stronger and colder.

The jetty called 1905 was a 300-metre walk from the restaurant with fantastic views over the ocean. The food and the wine were perfect. Of course, the oysters were on my hit list, and I ate a dozen of them myself. Matteo is an oyster lover, too, and we agreed they were some of the finest oysters we had ever had. He is also a wine lover and ordered some pleasant wines for the evening.

It was a happy evening, with lots of jokes, photos and friendly banter. Everyone made the effort to dress up, and all the women looked stunning. Unfortunately, it was soon time to leave and re-board the bus that would take us back to our guest house. It was now even colder than when we arrived. We left the restaurant and started on our 300-metre walk back to the bus, shivering.

In the morning, the guest house provided a full breakfast while Martina, Mila, Ella and I waited for our transport to the dolphin and seal cruise. The journey from the guest house to the pier, which was in Walvis Bay, took only about 30 minutes. We arrived in plenty of time for our cruise on a beautiful catamaran. It was a pleasant sunny morning for walking along the docks while waiting for our departure. The girls looked in some souvenir shops and outdoor stalls.

I was on a mission to try to phone the guest house without a sim card. (My South Africa sim card did not work in Namibia). I had forgotten to hand in my laundry. So I put my resourceful hat on and bought an espresso and a bottle of water. The girl who served me asked if I would like to come back for lunch later.

"Maybe. I'll see how hungry I am when I get back from the cruise. By the way, can I use your phone to make a local call?"

"Yes, of course. Who did you want to call?" I did not know the number of the guest house, and needed wi-fi to search for the number.

"Do you mind if I have the password to your wi-fi, please?"

She gave me the password so that I could look up the phone number for the guest house. I showed her the number, and she dialled it for me. When they answered it was a very bad line, and I could not understand them. So, I just said, "If you can hear me, I have forgotten to hand in my laundry this morning. My room is number three. Would you mind collecting it for me, please?" I hoped they could hear me as we were leaving the next day.

After the phone call I said thank you and asked to see the lunch menu to show that I might be interested in coming back for lunch. I paid for the coffee and water, said goodbye, and walked along the pier to meet the girls at the ticket office for the cruise.

Once we were on board the catamaran, the crew gave us a safety briefing and a talk about the marine life around Swakopmund. The departure pier was in amongst the shipping wharfs, giving it an industrial atmosphere as we headed out to sea. To my surprise I saw a semi-submersible oil rig near the wharf, and I could see a supply yard with some stored drilling equipment. I did not feel as excited as I used to, as I had been out of that industry for ten years.

Semi-submersible oil rig near Swakopmund

As we motored out of the harbour, we were offered "sailor's coffee", which was actually some sort of sweet rum. Most of us had a glass. I had my glass, Martina's half glass, and another full glass. The crew said, "The more you drink, the more dolphins you will see."

While we were drinking the "coffee" a seal managed to jump on board and slide around the deck as one of the crew fed it some fish. Then a pelican flew in and was fed fish as well. It was a pretty good show, and the creatures were very friendly.

As we increased speed heading further out to sea, the temperature started dropping, and my trusty hoody again came in handy. We passed a floating oyster farm where dozens of seals were either swimming around or resting on the floating drums. Further on past the oyster farm was a peninsula with hundreds of seals. Some were on the beach, and some on the concrete landing in front of the jetty. The chorus from the seals was like nothing I had ever heard before.

Sadly, as I looked beyond the seals on the beach, I saw dozens and dozens of dead seals on the sand. They were mostly small ones, but there were some larger ones, too. The explanation was that the great white sharks only transit these waters and do not feed there, resulting in an over-population of the seals, with not enough food for them. However, I have not found any evidence to support the crew's explanation. I have never seen so many dead animals in one area, and it was very disturbing.

Seals seen from the boat

After leaving the seals, we ventured further out to sea in hope of seeing some dolphins, but after thirty minutes or so, the crew announced that the dolphins were not around that morning. I guess the rum failed to have the effect we all wanted! We made a course back to the distant shore while the crew prepared lunch for us. I estimate there were at least 25 passengers on board. The seating area at the stern near the cockpit was adequate for most of us to sit around the well-presented table. Inside the cabin there was more space, but it was taken up by the crew preparing the food. Some of the passengers made do with sitting on top of the cabin under the boom and main mast. The sun was shining, and the water was blue. What a perfect way to spend lunch.

The lunch was outstanding: table service with flowing champagne, fresh oysters and canapes. The South African oyster has a taste all on its own. My favourite oyster is the Tasmanian oyster, but the South African oyster is very similar.

During the trip back to shore a couple of seals followed us while a crew member fed them fish, making them jump out of the water. One seal managed to climb on board while we were motoring along and lay on the rear steps. The seals put on a pretty good show. One passenger who had a bit too much champagne and beer wanted to touch one of the seals and was repeatedly asked not to touch them. I think the crew were quite annoyed with him and were happy to see him leave once we docked.

We all disembarked, very pleased with our tour, and walked along the wharf to our respective modes of transport. The four of us boarded our minibus, thinking we were the only passengers again, but more and more people started to board, too. Most of the passengers were Germans, and very loud. I wrote a message on my phone with my stylus pen and gave it to Ella who was sitting diagonally behind me: "Are they weird ones?"

A few days before, she had explained to me that most Germans on holiday are weird and loud, although she and her sister Mila are German. She wrote a reply on my phone which said, "Yes, they are definitely weird ones." Perhaps in the eyes of a 19-year-old and a 22-year-old, most people are weird.

We were the last passengers to be dropped off, and the four of us decided to go to our rooms for a rest. I rested until my phone was fully charged and then went for a slow walk while nursing my swollen toe. I was on the lookout for a local sim card. When I purchased my sim card in Cape Town I failed to realise that it would not work in the other countries we were visiting. I just assumed it would work all over Africa but this was not the case. Thankfully, everywhere we had been so far had free wi-fi.

After searching for some time, I failed to find an outlet that sold sim cards, and made my way to the beach back to the same bar in the cove I had visited before. Matteo and Liam were already sitting at a table. So I joined them and told them about our trip on the catamaran. Matteo had not booked any activities and had spent the day exploring the town. Liam had just returned from his sand boarding activity and had a great time. They stayed for another beer, and I invited them to another bar for dinner close to the guest house. While looking for a sim card I had found a bar called The Old Sailor. They said they would meet me there later. They paid their bill, and then they both left. I stayed for a couple of more beers while sorting out photos on my phone.

From the outside, The Old Sailor did not look very salubrious, but the sample menu looked good. As I walked in, I was pleasantly surprised by the furnishings and the ambience. There were quite a few people scattered around, sitting at tables or at the bar. I ordered a Tafel lager and found a small table to sit at. One of the waitresses presented me with a menu, which was huge. The more I looked through it, the more perplexed I became.

I noticed Anesu walking into the bar, and I managed to get his attention. He walked over and joined me.

"I'm ordering some food for myself and Kondjeni to take back to the guest house," he said.

The same waitress then presented Anesu with the menu. While Anesu was looking at the selections, I asked for two beers.

We talked for a while about how the trip was going, and about the passengers. He was very happy with everyone apart from one or two individuals. I agreed with him. We talked more about each other's home lives, his children, and what he would do once the tour finished.

I noticed Liam sitting at a table working on his laptop. He glanced up and gave us a wave but did not join us. Matteo eventually joined Anesu and me, and we had a couple of more beers before ordering some food. Anesu's order arrived first, and he said that he was leaving to take the food back to Kondjeni. Matteo and I enjoyed each other's company over some wine with our meals.

The next morning after breakfast we met Anneliese, a new passenger from Germany, who would be joining us for the rest of the tour. As I shook hands with her, I noticed how we held each other's gaze for a few seconds longer than normal. She had beautiful friendly eyes.

Once we were all on board the bus, Anesu spoke to us about the day's trip. We would touch the notorious Skeleton Coast before turning north-east toward Brandberg to stop and hike to the White Lady rock paintings. Finally, we would travel further to Uis.

It was a relatively cool morning when we left Swakopmund at 7.45. As we travelled along the coastline, I noticed a couple of more anchored oil rigs not far from the shore, along with groups of beach-casting fishermen. We stopped and walked on the beach to look at the shipwreck, *Zelia India.* The surf was quite punishing and continued to pound the ship's remains. Some of us became quite creative with our photography.

Surprisingly, there were people living on the beach close to the shipwreck. Before we left some of us gave them the snacks we had.

As we left the coast and headed inland, the weather became warmer, and the land began to change to the familiar desert landscape. We stopped in a café in Uis for coffee. After Uis, we passed through several small villages, stopping a few times to give drinking water to the villagers. Apparently, they belong to the Himba Tribe that lives in the desert.

There was a precarious moment where Kondjeni needed to negotiate a dry river crossing that was soft due to rain that had fallen overnight in the area. There was nothing he could do but to reverse and take a run-up to cross the soft, damp sandy river. It went well, and he received a round of applause from everyone.

Village on the way to Uis

As we were approaching Brandberg and the White Lady rock paintings, the land changed even more to a rockier landscape with high cliffs and interesting rock formations.

The rock paintings were in part of the Brandberg National Park, and the entrance fee was included with the tour. Everybody went for the hike with the guide, except for me as my gout was too painful to do a two-hour hike. I remained behind with Anesu and Kondjeni and helped prepare lunch.

After just one hour Ella and Mila arrived, totally exhausted. Martina appeared shortly after, and I think she was on the brink of dehydration. The temperature setting on my trusty Tissot watch displayed 37 degrees in the shade.

It had been more than two hours since the others had left, and we decided to start eating lunch. Shortly after, the rest of the group returned, also totally exhausted. After they cooled off, they ate lunch, and we all sat around chatting for a while. The leftovers from lunch were given to the people working at the national park.

After everything was cleaned and packed, we again boarded the bus and drove to our accommodation, the Brandberg White Lady Lodge. However, when Anesu went into Reception to obtain our keys, he came back to the bus to tell us we were at the wrong lodge. It was a slow and rough track back to the main dirt road. Once we had turned onto the main dirt road, we made our way back to Uis and our correct accommodation, the Brandberg Camping Lodge. I think all the tented people requested an up-grade to rooms, except for Martina who chose to use her tent. The activities and the drive consumed nine hours and 15 minutes, after travelling only 193 kilometres. The swimming pool was the first stop for everyone except for Leon and me. We opted to sit at a table in the shade at the bar with cold beers, overlooking the pool.

After an hour or so it was time to eat, and we walked to the camping area where Anesu had prepared some sort of stew for dinner. As Anneliese is a vegetarian, he had prepared a special meal for her.

After the meal, we discussed the next day's trip, which was going to be a short day, travelling to the edge of Etosha game park. Matteo, Leon and I walked back to the bar for a few wines. I think this is where I became a white wine drinker.

We all met for breakfast in the lodge and ordered eggs. The poor waitress was trying to memorise all the orders, and I wondered why she did not write them down. Some wanted their eggs over-easy, some sunny-side-up, some soft scrambled, and some well-done scrambled. After my order was forgotten, I had to wait longer for my sunny-side-up eggs. I sat with Brad, Carol and Anneliese. Somehow, we got onto the subject of energies and mental health. Anneliese showed me an app she uses for her mental health. I downloaded it and continued to use it throughout the trip.

We left Uis around 8.00 am. The gravel road was in good condition, and we made excellent time, stopping only once. To my surprise there were warning signs about elephants on the road. I think this area is well-travelled as there were several small roadside shelters that were selling cloth bags, bracelets and scarves. We only stopped at one and spent about thirty minutes looking at all their products.

We left the gravel road and turned onto the bitumen highway which took us to Outjo where we stopped for fuel, coffee and snacks. After we had parked and disembarked the bus, we were suddenly surrounded by children asking for money. Women with no tops on, showing their boobs, stood in the background. I think this is the normal way they dressed. The men tried to sell us souvenirs, but we made no purchases.

As I had run out of anti-inflammatory pills for my gout, I took the opportunity to find a chemist. I brought along my empty anti-inflammatory packet from Australia. I was grateful that they had exactly what I wanted, with the same ingredients.

Stalls on the way from Uis to Etosha

I walked next door to the supermarket to have a look around and decided to buy some treats for the children. I met Matteo in one of the aisles, and I told him what I was buying for the children. I explained that it would be better to buy them food than to give them money. He agreed and joined me in buying food and toys for them.

After our purchases we found a café. I had an espresso and a meat pie! We walked back to the bus, but it was still locked and Anesu was not there. While we waited, we handed out the food and toys to the women and children. However, then the men asked us why we were giving things to those kids when they had kids at home that needed food as well. I had the uneasy feeling that they were getting a little bit angry. Thankfully, things did not get any more heated.

When the rest of the group eventually arrived, they too were approached by the men asking for money. Anesu and Liam ignored them and chose to have their photo taken with the topless women! We got some great photos of them posing with the women, with wide smiles.

We left Outjo with men, women and children waving us goodbye. Our journey took us to our next destination and accommodation, the Eldorado. We would stay there for the next two nights, relaxing by the pool and the bar and travelling on a game drive.

Eldorado lies approximately six kilometres from the gates of Etosha game park. We arrived at 1.40 pm, after travelling for five hours and 40 minutes. As the trip was only 335 kilometres, it was a very easy day, travelling mostly on bitumen.

The accommodated people made use of the swimming pool and the bar for the afternoon. Anneliese and I had rooms next to each other. I thought this was a bit coincidental, but perhaps it was because we were the only single accommodated guests. Who knows?

My room was very rustic but modern. The main bedroom and bathroom were separated by three-quarter-height rock walls. Again, there were no wall plugs next to the bed to charge my phone.

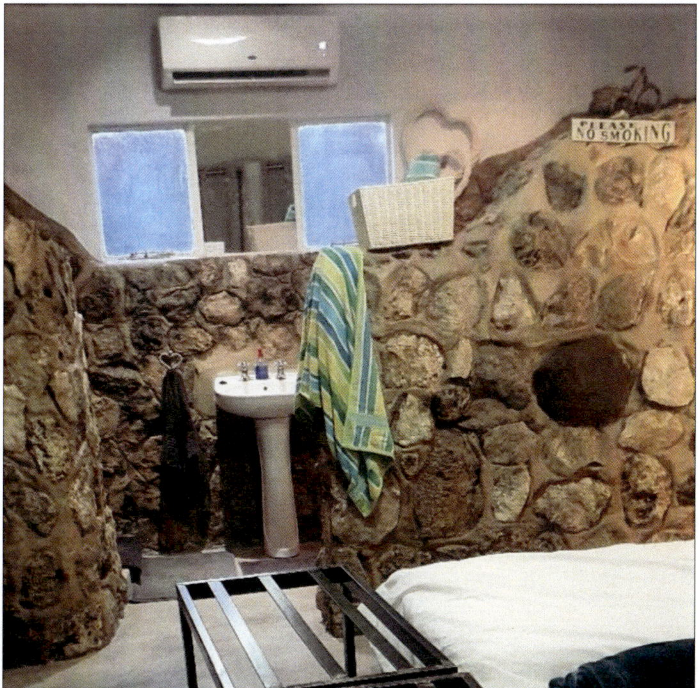

My room at Eldorado

The tented people joined us at the pool, as usual. Even though we were separated by the "tented" and "accommodated" labels, we were always together in the evenings and in the mornings.

The walk to the camping area for dinner was very slow due to the rocky path playing havoc with my toe. I continually told myself the gout was getting better!

I cannot remember what we had for dinner, but I am sure it was enjoyable! I went back to the bar and sat with Leon, Carol and Brad. Leon and I had a pretty good conversation, but Carol and Brad were engrossed in their phones. I said goodnight and took a glass of wine back to my room.

We started early the next day, meeting the open-sided 4 x 4 at 6.30 am and then driving into Etosha game park. It was frickin' cold! I was so glad I had brought my hoody. We needed two open-sided 4 x 4 vehicles, and I was with Liam, Martina, Matteo and Anneliese. The other vehicle took Steve, Sue, Ella and Mila. I was glad I was not in that vehicle! Leon, Brad and Carol stayed on Cynthia with Anesu and Kondjeni who took them on roads, looking for animals. They were unable to travel on the narrow tracks where the open-sided 4 x 4 vehicles can go.

It was an awesome day! I had never experienced anything like it. Being in an open-sided 4 x 4 vehicle and coming across springboks, giraffes, zebras, wildebeest, rhinoceros, a lion, impala and elephants! They were glorious to see, but I think the most majestic were the huge white elephant and the lion! I mean, holy shit! We stalked the lion for quite some time, and the guide would continually say to us, "Be patient. He will come to us." The lion was in the long grass, and every so often if we were quick enough, we could see his head pop up through the grass. The guide also said, "It is getting hotter now. He will move to find some shade."

Well, that shade was a lonely old tree in the middle of nowhere, close to where we were stalking him. Sure enough, the lion slowly rose to his feet and ever so slowly started walking to the shade of the lonely old tree. It was such an unbelievable sight to see: a frickin' lion walking toward us and the tree! Such a majestic animal, and nothing like the books, encyclopedias or Google can convey! It was real and very close! As excited as I was (and we all were excited), we had to remain silent.

Lion at Etosha

Giraffe at Etosha

The white elephant was just as spectacular. It was not like the usual black elephants you see and ride in Thailand. This thing was huge and a bit scary. I think it was a little angry, but I could not be sure. It was flapping its huge ears and staring at us.

The safari drivers have UHF two-way radios in their vehicles. So, whenever a guide sees an animal of interest, he makes a call over the radio, and then the rest of the guides, along with their tourists, will join the site where the animal of interest was spotted.

Rhinoceros at Etosha

When we spotted the white elephant, we were the only vehicle there, and we took our time stalking it and taking photos. When all the other guides showed up with their vehicles full of tourists, it was pretty much game over. Thankfully, we were the first ones there. Even our guide said we were a very lucky group, as we had seen all the animals in the Etosha game park, and he called it a good day.

The guide drove us back to the Etosha resort where we met the rest of the group for lunch, which consisted of make-your-own wraps. After lunch, we met with the guide again, and left in search of more animals – namely, the leopard! It was a good afternoon trip, but we did not find the leopard. Instead, we found rhinoceros, which was again unbelievable! There they were, just the two of them, as we drove around the corner on the gravel road, thirty metres away in the bush. They stood still long enough for us to take photos and videos. To be this close to African animals is surreal. I am not sure if that is a word to use to describe my feelings but that is what I am using.

It was a full day in the game park, and I spent it with the people who had become my friends. We transferred back to Cynthia at the end of the day and arrived back at Eldorado at about 5.00 pm. It was the usual drinks at the bar, and swim in the pool before eating near the bus. Dinner consisted of barbequed chicken wings, beans and salad. I had bought a bottle of Sauvignon Blanc to share at dinner. Leon and Matteo joined me in finishing off the bottle. I started to pack up the chairs but then Leon said we would probably need them the next morning at breakfast.

"There will probably be dew overnight and the chairs will get wet," I commented.

After that comment, the four Germans started talking amongst themselves in rapid German. Then it occurred to me that they did not understand the word "dew" and were probably thinking I had said "Jews"! I had to quickly explain the meaning of the word "dew".

The next day, we would only travel 102 kilometres, and the trip would take five hours. After our cooked breakfast we all cleaned up as usual and put things away. We left Eldorado Lodge at 8.00 am. Our journey took us through Etosha game park along the Etosha Pan, before turning south and eventually finishing at Tsumeb. We stopped several times during the journey to photograph animals: wildebeest, jackals, vultures, giraffes and dozens of zebras. We stopped and filmed a rhinoceros crossing the road. It looked like it was going to attack a small car in front of us! It was the highlight of our short trip. Of course, Brad would be talking loudly above us, all saying something like, "Look! Rhinoceros! Look!"

Rhinoceros crossing the road

We stopped at an information facility on the edge of the Etosha Pan which had toilets but they were unuseable due to the stench! We all just peed in the bush.

Looking out over the pan, we thought we could see water, but in fact it was just a mirage. I had never seen a mirage before, and it took a bit to convince me, but Anesu was positive it was a mirage.

We arrived in Tsumeb in overcast and drizzly conditions. Our accommodation was the Kpferquelle Resort, where we were met with glasses of sparkling wine, and an explanation of the resort's lay-out. We walked to our rooms which were quite a distance from Reception and up-hill, past the Olympic-sized swimming pool. I met the hotel porters at my room who delivered my bag on a golf buggy. Coincidentally, Anneliese was right next door again! The tented people all had rooms that were again included. The rooms were very modern and luxurious.

After I looked around the grounds, I met everyone at Cynthia in the camping area, where lunch was being prepared by Anesu.

After lunch, Matteo and I decided to take a short walk to the shops to buy some beer and biltong, but they told us beer could not be sold after 2.00 pm. We decided to meet at the bar in an hour while he used the laundry facilities. I watched some TV in my room. It was a bit of a novelty and felt a little strange, as. I had not watched TV for a while.

The sun started to shine as I walked to the bar where Matteo was already waiting for me. Leon and Martina joined us a little later and we enjoyed a few beers until it was time to get ready for dinner. We re-convened at 7.00, and the others joined our reserved table in the dining room where we were served several types of pizzas and salads to share.

After everyone had eaten, some people said goodnight and left to walk back to their rooms. Only Martina, Matteo, Anneliese, Ella and I remained to have a few more drinks. Our main topic of conversation was relationships, and what we looked for in a potential partner, and what is an acceptable age gap. It was an interesting topic, with varied responses.

In the morning, we left our bags by the front door of our rooms for the hotel porters to collect and take down to the bus while we ate breakfast. It was a sunny morning, and the day ahead was all on bitumen. We left Tsumeb and our beautiful resort at 7.40, heading for Divindu via Grootfontein for fuel and snacks. There were few photo opportunities, and I think we only stopped twice for bushy bushy.

At 3.15 pm we arrived at our accommodation on the Kavango River, making it a journey of seven hours and 35 minutes to travel over 513 kilometres. The lodge setting was picturesque enough, but the rooms themselves were very average, to say the least. I did not want to shower for fear of getting some sort of tinea, and I slept with clothes on for fear of catching something from the sheets. This lodge was definitely the worst one so far, especially after staying in a beautiful resort the previous night.

On top of it all, the power was out, the wi-fi was down, and the beer was warm. However, the setting was quite picturesque, especially the walk from the rooms down the hill toward the waterfront, bar, pool and restaurant. The first thing I asked them to do was to stock some beer and ice in an Esky, and they happily did just that.

While some people sat by the pool and swam, some of us sat at a table near the bar drinking beer. Now and then we could hear a groaning sound coming from the river. Someone said that it sounded like a hippopotamus. Little did we know that the river was full of hippos.

As the sun began to set, people took the opportunity to take some photos. Then, around 7.30 pm the power was restored, and the wi-fi came to life. We were then seated at our reserved table and served dinner: beef stroganoff and chicken wings, which were very nice.

We all turned in shortly after dinner. The tented people again had rooms. I stayed up for a while at the bar watching yet more TV – a soccer game, even though I did not know who was playing – but I needed to charge my phone as the battery was nearly flat.

The next morning we had a bit of a late start, but it was a pleasant morning having breakfast cooked for us on a pontoon boat. A woman who was positioned at the back of the boat next to the skipper was taking orders for cooked eggs. There were also fruit, cereal, plunger coffee, ham and cheese, and toast.

Hippopotamuses on the Kavango River

We motored around looking for hippos and found several herds. We were all in awe at the sight of these majestic and placid creatures. Contrary to what people would have us believe, these animals did not attack us. They would watch us, submerge, and reappear again in a peaceful manner. Apparently, though, if you fell in the water they would not hesitate to attack, as you would be close to their territory and flailing your arms on the surface. The only way to escape from a hippo attack is to swim deep as they have very poor eyesight.

It was a great morning, but after docking on the riverbank it was time to pack up. We met the bus near our rooms with our bags and finally left the lodge at 9.40 in the direction of Maun in Botswana. The trip would take us eight hours and 10 minutes, travelling 425 kilometres.

Botswana

We stopped to have our passports stamped with exit stamps from Namibia and entry stamps into Botswana. An official entered the bus and inspected our food supply to make sure we were not carrying any meat. Apparently, Botswana is very strict regarding foot and mouth disease. This took about 30 minutes but was fine because we made use of the free wi-fi.

Almost instantly after crossing the border, the roads deteriorated badly, with huge potholes that slowed us down considerably. Kondjeni did very well not to drive into them. Again, the day did not provide any good photo opportunities.

Anesu and Kondjeni found a gravel track leading off the main pot-holed road, and we took the opportunity to stop and make a quick lunch of hotdogs. We only drove onto the start of the track to stay off the main road and did not venture any further. We happily disembarked the bus only to find that the soil smelled of pee! Also, the ground was dotted with huge prickles that had the potential to pierce shoes and feet. The barbs were 50 millimetres long and very strong. Despite our surroundings we were happy just to be off the bus after travelling on the rough road. Unfortunately, our reprieve did not last long as we had left Divindu late, resulting in a late arrival into Maun.

Our departure after lunch was delayed because the table slide trouble we had at Walvis Bay had become worse, most likely from the potholes, and we were unable to slide the tables under the bus. Thankfully, Kondjeni had a small tool kit but lacked a pair of pliers. The Leatherman multitool I had brought with me saved the day by contributing to the temporary repairs needed to continue on our way.

We stopped one more time in a small town to withdraw some local Botswana cash (pula) which was needed for tipping and for purchases in some places that did not have credit card facilities. After about 30 minutes, we continued on our way and finally reached Maun and our accommodation, the Maun Lodge, at 5.30 pm.

Everyone had their own rooms once again, and check-in was seamless. Our registration forms had already been prepared and set out on the counter ready for us to sign, along with a welcome drink of fruit juice.

I carried my bag to my room, sorted out some laundry and brought it to Reception, being informed that it would be ready by that evening. It was already after 6.00 and time for the first beer of the day at the bar. It was my first Botswanan beer called

Louis Lager. It came a close second to my favourite South African beer, Windhoek Lager.

Leon joined me, followed by Matteo and Anneliese. We ordered more drinks and proceeded to browse the menu. We asked for a table for four people, but as we looked for a table, we noticed a long table with a card saying, "Roaming Safaris". The four of us took our seats, and slowly the rest of the group started arriving to join us.

I ordered a steak, while Anneliese, Liam, Martina and Matteo ordered the river fish. Apparently, the fish is famous in African cuisine. We were all pleased with the food, drinks and service.

A solo DJ playing was playing familiar Reggae music in the background. The theme song of the tour was "Jambo Bwana", which is an old Kenyan pop song that Anesu introduced to us. Martina approached the DJ to ask if he could play "Jambo Bwana". When the song played, Martina, Anneliese, Liam and Carol were dancing in the middle of the restaurant while the rest of the restaurant watched and joined in the chorus.

After a few more drinks and good conversations around the table, people slowly started returning to their rooms. Ella, Mila, Leon, Giuseppe, Carol and Steve needed to be up early the next morning to board their scenic flight.

As Matteo and I were the last ones left, we moved to the bar to browse the wine list. We ended up buying a bottle of Sauvignon Blanc and talking for a while longer. Conversations with Matteo were always entertaining and interesting. He was just 23 years old, had spent some time in the Swiss army, and was a chemist in a brewery. He loved classical piano, was a Formula One enthusiast, and was very knowledgeable about wines and cigars.

The wines the night before helped me sleep through until 8.00 am. We all needed a sleep-in after our early morning starts over the previous two weeks.

I organised some clothes and essentials into a backpack as we would change vehicles during the day and leave our main big bags here in Maun, locked up on Cynthia with Kondjeni. I walked downstairs to have breakfast in the restaurant and was looking forward to eating alone and easing into the day. I ordered scrambled eggs from the chef and added some mushrooms, tomatoes and ham to my plate. As I turned to walk back to my table, I met Sue. She had not gone with her husband Steve on the scenic flight that morning. Of course, she joined me, and we made friendly chit-chat over breakfast. Martina had returned from the swimming pool and joined us for breakfast as well.

While I was talking with Matteo the night before, we had looked online trying to find cigars in Maun. We found a shop in a mall not far from the lodge that might sell cigars. We wanted to smoke cigars around the next campfire with some nice wine.

I asked Martina and Sue if they would like to come on a walk with me to the mall, but they both declined. Just as I was about to stand and leave the restaurant, the six people from the early morning scenic flight walked into the restaurant. My peaceful breakfast had been obliterated.

Their appraisal of the flight was not exactly captivating. I got the impression that it was not worth the money or the early-morning start. The consensus was that the altitude was too high to see any animals, but the scenery was impressive from that height.

I took my leave of the group and walked to Reception. I asked the woman on duty for directions to the mall, and if it was far to walk.

"It is not far to walk, but you should take a taxi as it can be dangerous to walk there," she advised. I contemplated the thought of catching a taxi, the waiting time for the taxi to come, and the time required to find some cigars.

"How long will it take to walk?"

"Only about ten minutes."

"OK, I think I will walk. Thank you." I walked to the front gate and looked at the highway I needed to cross and walk along. I asked the guard at the gate, "How do I cross the highway?"

"You can just cross, sir."

He was right. The highway was not very busy at all. I thanked him and proceeded to cross the highway to the footpath on the other side that would take me to the mall.

A section of the highway spanned over a wide dried-up river. I wondered if the rainfall in this area would ever bring the river back to its full glory. As I walked over the dried-up river, I saw that sections of the concrete barriers had been smashed, leaving large gaps. The danger was that I might fall through onto the sand below, or be injured by the protruding steel reinforcing as I walked past them.

I reached the carpark for the mall and negotiated my way to the entrance. Once I was inside, I found a myriad of stores ranging from electronics stores to food outlets, and to clothing and grocery shops. I found one shop that sold cigars, but they were in thin packets.

My walk back to the lodge was uneventful. I received a friendly wave and a smile from the guard at the main gate as I passed the lodge on the way to my room. I retrieved my bags and met the others at the bus. We boarded the bus, locked our big bags into the bus lockers and started to leave the lodge. We made it as far as the exit where it joins onto the highway, when Liam yelled out to Kondjeni in his broad Irish accent, "I've left me swimmers behind! Can we go back please?"

Everyone groaned as Kondjeni reversed up the long driveway back to the parking area. Anesu climbed down from the cab and opened the main door for Liam. As Liam was disembarking through the main door, a few people yelled out to him to check the bus locker for his swimmers.

"I've already checked, and they are definitely not in there," he replied.

After ten minutes or so, Liam returned without his swimmers.

"Fuck me, I've searched everywhere. They're lost." Liam searched his locker again when he reboarded the bus. "Oh, here they are!" he exclaimed. Everyone let out a groan and had a little chuckle at his expense.

We finally left Maun Lodge at 10.40 am for the short drive to meet the modified 12-seat, open-sided 4 x 4 safari vehicle near the airport. We all disembarked the bus carrying a bag each to last us for two nights at a camp site. We were introduced to Numba, our new guide for the next three days. He was a burly man with a friendly smile, and once we were all seated in the vehicle, along with Anesu, he spoke to us about the importance of having enough water during our journey to the Kwai conservation area, and about the animals we might see once we arrived at the conservation area and what not to do when we encountered them.

With me in the front seat next to Numba, we waved goodbye to Kondjeni and left Maun at 11.05 am. After about an hour of travel along the bitumen road we had to pull over and roll down the plastic screen. I helped Numba zip the plastic screen closed to stop the wind punishing the passengers seated behind me.

The road turned to dust and gravel, with numerous crossings that had evidence of vehicles being bogged. They had left behind deep ruts and branches that were used to recover the bogged vehicles.

After about two and a half hours of travelling we found a shady tree where we stopped for a pre-prepared lunch of sandwiches, apples and cake. It was also a good opportunity for bushy bushy, but when I looked at Liam, I saw it was too late for him: he had a large wet patch around his groin area. I felt he should have asked Numba to stop earlier to prevent his embarrassment.

The road did not get any better, but the scenery changed when Numba drove off the main gravel road onto a two-wheeled track that was marked by an inverted wine bottle placed on a branch. Then came another 40 minutes of slow driving, scraping over-hanging tree branches, and passing through thick reed-covered water crossings. The ground was black mud but thankfully it was not flinging into the vehicle.

It was a long and exciting day, and we arrived at our campsite in the Moremi Reserve at 4.00 pm. As we drove into the camp, in the distance I could see people walking through the long reeds and wondered what they were doing out there. When Numba stopped the vehicle in front of the main marquee, I asked Numba about the people walking in the reeds.

"They are not walking. They are standing on canoes and pushing themselves along with long poles. We are going to meet them soon."

The camp site consisted of the main marquee where we would be served dinner, breakfast and drinks. The kitchen was located approximately 25 metres from the marquee, which was enveloped by tarpaulin walls. There were several glamping tents for accommodated people. On the other side of the glamping tents were the basic tents for the tented people, who shared a long drop toilet and a bush shower. Inside the glamping tents we had our own chemical toilets and bush showers, with beds and racks to place our clothes on. The flooring consisted of thick waterproof plastic that zipped all around, preventing any creepy crawlies from entering. It even had a bedside table and a lamp that was solar-powered, as were the room light and bathroom light. It was a well-set-up camp site.

The main marquee at the Kwai Conservation Park in the Moremi Reserve

We did not stop for long at the camp, and after a quick leg stretch, we were asked to climb back onboard the 4 x 4. Numba drove us to a meeting point amongst the reeds where the "canoe people" were waiting for us. We disembarked from the 4 x 4 and received a warm welcome from the head canoe guide. He proceeded to talk to us about the area and the animals, and how to sit in the canoes. After his talk, we divided into couples and chose a canoe. The "pole men" were already standing at the rear of the canoes waiting for people to board. Once two people were seated in the canoe, the pole man pushed off the bank with his pole. Some of us needed to get out to help push the canoe off the bank.

The water was only approximately one metre deep and very clean and clear. At first, it was an eerie feeling to be in a canoe surrounded by tall reeds, following a channel of water with a strange man standing behind you with a long pole! However, as I settled in with Matteo and started to take in the natural beauty and ambience, it felt pretty cool! The man standing behind me with the big pole was no longer an imaginary bad man, but a very nice young man who told us numerous tribal stories of himself and his family, and how he grew up in this part of Africa.

As he continued to push Matteo and me through the water, I noticed the lily pads, the water flowers and the fish beneath us. I was becoming so chilled out, until I heard some animal noises. I asked our pole man what that noise was.

"They are hippos. But they will not come to us. We are away from their territory."

We enjoyed a relaxing cruise through the water, but the pole men and guide decided to have a rest and pushed our canoes up a bank where we were allowed to disembark and have a walk around. On the bank was a skull of a hippopotamus. The main guide gave us a talk about the skull, and how it came to be there. Basically, the hippo had been sick and then it was preyed upon by other animals.

The pole men followed the same channel of water back to the meeting point where Numba was waiting for us. Along the way, I found myself being mesmerised by the flowing underwater vegetation. The water was so clear, it was almost invisible, and seeing the flowing vegetation made me feel like we were floating on air!

Numba greeted us with a welcoming wave and a huge, white-toothed smile as our canoes came into view. One by one, we docked our canoes onto the bank and disembarked. Some of us handed tips to the pole men, and some of us did not.

As the pole men poled their way out of the reeds toward their homes, we turned to look at Numba.

Open-sided Landcruiser

"Everybody on board, and we go," he said. I looked at the roof rack and asked if I could ride back to the camp on the roof. He hesitated for a while.

"Yes, you can. Just don't fall off." Some of the other people heard me ask Numba, and as soon as Numba said yes, four people were already climbing up the ladder to the roof rack on the Toyota Landcruiser.

The Landcruiser had been modified from its original specifications. It had at least a 750 mm chassis extension, a Gross Vehicle Mass upgrade, and its roof removed. The interior was also modified to accommodate 14 people including the driver, but it still had the original manual front wheel locking hubs. Funnily enough, it was still the original Toyota sandy colour.

Numba drove us on the five-kilometre muddy track back to the camp with Anneliese, Ella, Matteo, Brad, Martina and me riding on the roof rack. We had a great view, and we saw the pole people in the background going wherever it was they were going. It still looked like they were walking on land. When Numba parked the car at the camp, all the staff were waiting to greet us, with the campfire roaring away.

After we disembarked from the 4 x 4 we sat in camp chairs around the fire, and the camp boss, Celia, welcomed us all and talked about the proceedings over the coming two nights. Numba in turn talked to us about the animals in the area. He said there would be animals roaming within the camp at night, and what not to do if we were confronted with a wild animal in the middle of the night. Basically, we should not leave our tents at night.

After the staff had spoken to us, we were shown to our tents and were allowed enough time to unpack and settle in before coming back to the fire for drinks. Yet again, Anneliese was in the tent next to mine.

During drinks, one of the staff approached me and said that my shower was ready. This meant that they had added enough hot and cold water for a warm bush shower in my tent.

It was a very pleasant shower, and the wooden pallet floor under the shower was a nice touch as it let the water drain away. I made my way by torchlight back to the main marquee and the campfire. I sat around the fire for a while until dinner was ready.

We sat in random seats along the long table. As it turned out, I was sitting with Anneliese, Martina and Matteo. For some reason, wherever we sat for meals during the tour, we were always together or not too far from each other.

Celia announced that dinner was ready to be served, and that the women should bring their plates and serve themselves first from the food trays. The men followed after the women had finished dishing up their food, which was some sort of chicken stew accompanied by rice. Some of us went back for seconds as it was delicious, and the only food we had eaten all day was the sandwiches on the side of the gravel road.

After we finished dinner and the staff had taken away all the plates, Numba asked for our attention and again explained about camping etiquette around wild animals. He said that some animals might walk through the camp during the night. We were not to leave our tents during the night, and not to shine our torches on the animals, as this would either startle them or make them angry.

When Numba finished addressing the group, we were free to order more drinks and sit around the fire, which was roaring by then. The weather was surprisingly cool, and the fire was quite welcoming. Some of us stayed for a while talking and drinking around the fire while others took themselves off to their tents. Martina, Matteo, Anesu, Leon and I had drinks around the fire until about 9.30. The day's travels took only five hours and 20 minutes over 124 kilometres, but we were all tired.

The next day was to be a day for animal spotting. Anneliese and I greeted each other outside our tents in the morning.

"That chemical toilet and I will never become friends!" she commented. I assumed that she had never used one before.

I met with Liam on the way to the marquee for breakfast, and he said that he had an upset stomach. It later transpired that Anneliese, Martina and Matteo also had upset stomachs. This was not the place to have stomach problems. Thankfully, I was fine for the whole trip.

After breakfast was served at 6.00 am, Numba drove us out of the campsite at 6.30 through the cool, reedy swamp lands for our morning safari. It seemed that Numba misjudged a section of the swamp, and we became bogged. Everyone moaned and groaned and suggested to Numba to try applying all sorts of 4 x 4 techniques. All the suggestions came from people, such as the professional people, who had never been bogged before!

Numba disembarked the 4 x 4 and walked to the rear of the vehicle to retrieve the kangaroo jack. As I knew exactly what he was going to do, I disembarked as well to help him. His plan was to jack the vehicle up and then place dry material under the wheels to enable some traction. Anesu also knew what the plan was and disembarked the 4 x 4 to help Numba and me. We needed some dry material, and the only things around were low-lying trees. The three of us walked to the nearest trees, broke off some limbs and managed to find dead tree limbs on the ground. Once we carried the limbs back to the vehicle, we placed the limbs under the jacked-up wheels. The wheels needed to be jacked up one at a time.

Everyone else remained in the vehicle except for Brad who walked with us and half-heartedly picked up some limbs from the ground. I returned to the vehicle at one point and Carol asked where Brad was.

"He's over there supervising," I replied.

I then asked the group if they were looking out for lions instead of watching us work. I don't think anyone thought to look for lions.

My feet, thongs and hands were covered in mud, but there was no choice: we had to get the vehicle out. After about an hour of jacking and placing limbs under the wheels, we were ready to give it a try. Numba drove out of the bog with no resistance whatsoever. Everyone shouted out a big cheer. We remounted the kangaroo jack, climbed back into the 4 x 4 and continued on our way.

During our bumpy ride, an elephant crossed our path. As instructed by Numba, we remained very quiet and obtained dozens of photos and videos of the majestic animal. During our silent photo session, the elephant decided to walk closer to our vehicle and cross the road. It was both scary and exciting at the same time. Its eyes looked at us all as it crossed in front of our 4 x 4. Such an experience!

Injured zebra in the Moremi Reserve

We left it in its natural habitat and drove further to find an injured zebra. It had a chunk of flesh hanging from its chest. It was likely a wound from either a jackal or a hyena. The zebra looked despondent but not fazed at all by our presence. Numba said that it would probably look for a quiet place to die.

During our search for more animals, Martina suddenly yelled out, "I need to go bushy bushy!" I think she started climbing out of the vehicle with her roll of toilet paper even before it came to a stop. When she came back, she said in her thick Spanish accent, "It was an explosion!"

One of the professional people suggested that the illness was due to the fish that the four of them had eaten at the Maun Lodge Restaurant. Eating the fish meal seemed to coincide with their upset stomachs. Note to self: do not eat river fish!

Just before we stopped for morning tea, we crossed paths with a lonely giraffe, peacefully munching away on tree leaves. We took the time to silently watch the animal and take photographs, scanning every inch of the animal.

We drove away leaving it to continue eating while we searched for a shady tree of our own for morning tea. We had only tea, coffee and biscuits, but we were grateful for a leg stretch.

It was time to drive back to the camp. We arrived without getting bogged and without any more "explosions" at 11.50, with the friendly reminder that lunch would be ready at 12.10. As the next safari was due to depart at 3.30, after lunch almost everyone went to their tents to rest. I tried to rest in my tent, but it was much too hot. I do not know how everyone else managed to rest in steaming hot tents.

I ended up staying under the marquee in the breeze, while I continued with my writing. Anesu, Matteo and Leon joined me after a while, saying it was too hot to sleep in their tents. I had my map of Namibia out on the table. I was studying the roads we had taken and adding all the names of the people on the tour to the map. Leon was quite interested in what I was doing and asked to take a few photos of my map. Matteo looked like he was concentrating on not shitting himself, I think.

Gradually, the other people started showing up and getting ready for the afternoon safari. I told them that I was not attending the afternoon safari and preferred to stay at the camp and continue with my writing.

"I think that's a great idea," Anneliese said.

I thought she was going to stay and join me for some solitude. She was thinking about it, but she ended up going with the rest of the group. I was the only one who stayed behind when they all left in the 4 x 4.

I had a good feeling about being on my own and having an uninterrupted session with my diary. However, one of the staff members walked over from the kitchen and asked if I was all right.

"Yes, I'm fine. I'm just enjoying the solitude."

"You didn't want to go on the safari?"

"No, I went this morning, and that is enough."

As I continued to write, she kept interrupting and talking to me. I decided that there was no longer any point in trying to write when she wanted to have a conversation. So, I asked her to find a cold beer for me, and I closed my book and started talking to her. Her name was Lesh. She was a nice girl whose job was to clean and spray the tents and help in the kitchen. We seemed to get along well.

In between errands, she would come back to talk to me or ask if I would like another beer. Other staff members would also come by and ask if I was all right. Maybe they were not used to seeing people sitting alone!

After several hours, we started to question the arrival time of the second safari. It was already 7.00 pm and they had not returned. Lesh asked Celia about it, and she said they would return shortly and she was not worried. I was a little worried, as I kept remembering being bogged that morning. Maybe they were bogged again.

Then, at 7.45, the headlights of the 4 x 4 came into view. It was a customary greeting that all the staff would line up in front of the fire and sing a welcome song. I was standing with the staff in front of the fire trying to sing in my best African!

The returning group were given only 20 minutes to shower and return to the marquee for dinner. When they returned, they talked about their animal encounters over dinner and drinks. They had seen a hyaena with a cub.

After dinner it was the usual crowd sitting around the fire drinking, apart from Matteo, who was still suffering with stomach problems. It was our last night at the camp, and some of us made the most of it and drank more around the fire. Unfortunately, they closed the bar at 9.30.

I hoped that the drinks I had would help me sleep, but a lion close to our camp kept roaring all night, keeping me awake. It was only sporadic, but enough to make me aware of a lion at the camp. There were also hyaena and hippo noises.

Elephant in the Morimi Reserve

Regardless of how much sleep we had during the night, breakfast was at 6.00 am. At 6.30 we were all climbing into the 4 x 4 with the entire staff watching us. As we drove away, they all waved at us and wished us a safe journey. I looked at Lesh, and she stared at me as if to say, "I wish you weren't leaving."

The journey from the camp to the main gravel road was a lengthy 30 minutes or more of tackling swamps, overhanging limbs, and washed-out tracks. Along the way we encountered giraffes, elephants and a herd of hippos.

I still find it hard to believe that Martina asked Ella to plait her hair while we were looking at the herd of hippos! Suddenly, Martina had turned to Ella and said, "Can you do my hair?"

"Yes, of course."

Meanwhile, the rest of us were looking at the herd of hippos in the water.

As our journey took us closer to the end of the Kwai Conservation Area, we needed to complete a formality which involved all of us disembarking the 4 x 4 and walking to a check point where we had to stand in a tray with our shoes on. The tray was filled with some sort of cleansing solution.

After the cleansing, I noticed that the gravel road that we drove out on was not as bad as when we drove in. It was still rough, but it did not seem to take as long to travel it. However, it still took over four hours, meaning that we arrived in Maun at 11.15 am. We met Kondjeni and Cynthia and ate the burgers that the Kwai staff had prepared for us. Anesu was in a hurry, and insisted we eat on the bus as we drive. This did not make much sense as we drove not more than ten minutes to a mall to stop for supplies. We all made use of this time to search for a coffee shop. We found one easily, and it had free wi-fi to upload all our photos taken at Kwai, which did not have wi-fi.

After an hour or so, we meandered back to the bus and continued our route to Nata. All was going well until the police pulled Kondjeni over. Apparently, he was speeding, but they let him off. After another couple of hours of travelling, he was signalled to pull over again by different police. This time they fined him 1400 Pula, which is about $160 AUD. I guess we should have wished for more potholes! We had several bushy bushy stops along the way, and it was a long trip.

We finally arrived in Nata at 5.35 pm, making it an 11-hour day over 420 kilometres. Some of the people, namely the professional people, were very annoyed at the length of time on the road and were going to write to the tour company about it. Overall, we agreed that it was a very long time to sit on a bus, but approximately five hours of that time involved travel from the bush camp back to Maun.

Our accommodation in Nata was the Elephant Sands Lodge, a very nice, unique place. The cottages were quite a distance from the main lodge, and 4 x 4 transport was required at nighttime as there were animals roaming around. However, we did not see or hear any animals.

The accommodation was quite unusual. The cottages could be described as glamping tents on wooden platforms, but in fact, there had been quite a lot of work required to build the cottages. The roof and walls were canvas. The front door was a wooden door inside a wooden frame. Inside, the main room had a separate bathroom, with a fully functional shower, sink and toilet. All around the tent were canvas walls and zippered canvas windows.

After checking in and being driven to our rooms with our bags, we met at the main lodge by the pool and talked with Kondjeni about his speeding fines. He explained that the Botswana police are so corrupt that they move the speed limit signs to catch people speeding. We all chipped in to pay for his speeding fine because we knew he was actually not speeding.

The meal was included for the night, and we helped ourselves, except for the four people who were still feeling a little sick in the stomach. We could not see what we were eating as it was dark due to our late arrival, and there were no night lights around the place, but it was a good presentation, and it tasted delicious.

Some of us sat around the fire after dinner, but most went to their cabins. As usual, it was just Matteo and I at the bar until closing time, which was 9.00 pm. We were then shown to a 4 x 4 to take us to our rooms as it was lodge policy not to walk to our rooms at night.

In the morning, I carried my own bag to the bus at the camping area, where Anesu and Martina were already making breakfast for us. Matteo and Kondjeni were at the souvenir shop near Reception, picking up some last-minute souvenirs.

Eventually, the dishes were dried and put away, and we boarded the bus and left Nata at 8.15 am for an easy day on the road to Kasane. There was nothing worthy of a photo along the way, and we arrived at the Thebe River Lodge at 12.10 pm. The thatched roofing of the main building and accommodations gave it a typical African look. After checking in, we followed the under-cover U-shaped walkway leading to our rooms.

Anesu was busy cooking us lunch at the camping area as we were all settling into our rooms. He had previously organised for a person to meet us at the camp site with samples of t-shirts for purchase. There were so many colours and print styles to choose from that I changed my mind several times about the colour.

After we had eaten lunch and ordered our t-shirts, it was time for a rest as we were being picked up at 2.45 for another adventure. I did not have a sleep, but by the look of some of the people who embarked the bus, I think they must have had an afternoon siesta. Matteo and I prepared the Esky for our adventure before leaving the lodge. Anesu stayed behind to prepare and cook that night's meal while we drove to the jetty to meet the ferry. The departure time for the ferry was 3.15.

When we arrived at the jetty, everyone disembarked the bus. As usual, it was up to Matteo and me to carry the Esky, which was extremely heavy with everyone's drinks as well as ice. We managed to carry it along the rocking pontoons to board the pontoon boat, but not one person from our group offered to help. It was very disappointing. I think there were two other groups on board as well, from Roaming Safaris. So Matteo and I found a nice place on the back of the deck where we could sit and have the Esky between us. Also, it was close to the toilets.

We untied from the jetty to power upriver, and then we stopped at what looked like a three-way intersection of the river. The skipper left his controls at the rear of the boat, walked to the front, and talked about the river, the animals, and the need to hold onto our cameras as he was not jumping into the water to retrieve any personal items.

After his interesting talk, we thought we were going to power on with the tour, but he steered back to shore to another jetty. He said that he needed to obtain a permit to cruise along the Chobe River. We waited for approximately 20 minutes while he disembarked, walked to the station on the jetty, and then came back on board.

Crocodile on the Chobe River cruise

Finally, we were powering along the Chobe River, on the lookout for wildlife. The first wildlife we saw was a 3-metre crocodile very close to us. A maze of small river systems led into the main river, and I was glad that the skipper knew where he was going.

Around the next bend we encountered a herd of elephants on the banks. Some were swimming, some were eating, and some were eating and swimming at the same time. A baby elephant seemed to be playing in the water while the mother stood over it. Every time the baby tried to leave the water by crawling up the bank, the mother would push it back into the water. The skipper came in very close to the herd, allowing us the opportunity for photography. It was majestical to witness these animals in the wild, not behind bars, or acting frightened.

Elephants on the Chobe River

They were beautiful in sight and soul. I asked myself: who the fuck would want to slay these animals? I understand that they can cause mayhem in crops, but there must be a better way. Actually, these water elephants are very different from the ones we encountered in the bush. I can see how the bush ones can be more destructive as I have witnessed their destruction. Perhaps the water elephants are not as destructive. However, I am far from being an expert on elephants. I am just a tourist.

In the background of the elephant herd was a small herd of water buffalos. Unfortunately, they were too far away for any photographs or videos.

Hippopotamus eating grass on the Chobe River

We moved to another bank on the other side of the river and found a lonely hippo feeding on grass and weed. It was very fat, and did not look like it needed any more to eat, but it was like an eating machine! Nonstop eating! The hippos we saw on the Kavango river were always submerged. This one was on land and walking and eating. I could then see what a whole hippo looks like.

Baboons on the bank of the Chobe River

We started turning to make our way down the river to our original jetty. Along the way we spotted a group of baboons hanging around the base of a tree. It was not clear what the attraction of that particular tree was, but we came close enough to the baboons to take photos and videos. In the background were impala, feeding on grass. Further downriver, we stopped near another bank to witness some mongoose and guinea fowl frolicking around in the bush. We eventually docked at our departure jetty at 6.45 pm. Again, Matteo and I carried the Esky back to the bus, but at least it was somewhat lighter by then.

We arrived back at the lodge around 7.00. We all met at the bus camp site around 7.20 for our last meal together. The tour was coming to an end, and we could all feel it. There were only two days left together as a group.

Anesu had worked all afternoon preparing and cooking a fantastic last meal for us all. As he had not quite finished, Matteo and I helped with the last-minute barbeque chores. Apart from that, Anesu had done it all: everything was laid out, the tables were decorated, cutlery was on the tables, and the chairs were in place. It was an outstanding effort.

The only people who did not show up were Brad and Carol: they could not be bothered to share a last meal with us. Pretty piss-poor, man! I have no respect for them; they are just snobby, rich professionals who think they are better than anyone else, and the whole group, apart from the other professionals, thought the same way. Nevertheless, we all tucked in to the fine food Anesu had cooked, and we all washed up and put things away like we had always done for the previous three weeks.

We said our goodnights. I went to the outdoor bar, which had an interesting ambience. After a while Leon joined me. He stayed for one drink and then left to fill out his immigration forms for Zimbabwe. Anneliese walked into the bar and came straight toward me.

“Should we find a table?” she asked.

“Sure.” I looked around at a few tables, thinking that it was just going to be Anneliese and I, but then she said, “I think other people might be joining us.”

My thoughts of getting together with Anneliese were shattered once again! When Martina and Matteo entered the bar, Anneliese waved to them, and we all decided on a table. We ordered drinks and produced our immigration forms for Zimbabwe for the next day, and our Roaming Safaris customer survey forms. We all helped each other to fill in the forms. It was interesting as there were four people of different nationalities working our way through the forms: Swiss, German, Spanish and Australian. All the while, there was a group of loud males at another table, and this did not help our ability to communicate with each other.

After our forms were completed, we stayed for quite a while talking about many topics over quite a few drinks. I later learned that Anneliese was not a drinker and was drinking zero-alcohol Heineken. Martina, Matteo and I were sharing white wine. I think we drank at least two bottles among the three of us, as well as the drinks we had while filling in our forms. Thankfully, the loud people near our table had gone by then.

The waiter returned to our table several times insisting on refilling our glasses and feeding us with nuts. He turned to Matteo and asked, "Do you like the nuts?"

Matteo replied, "Yes, you have nice nuts." We all laughed at Matteo's expense.

The conversations the four of us had over drinks were quite personal, ranging from sex to relationships past and current, to what an ideal partner would be. Age gap in relationships was brought up several times as well. The consensus on big age gap relationships was that age should not matter. What should be a consideration is that if the woman is much younger, then the subject of having children should be discussed. Also, the subject of the ageing man being taken care of later in the relationship should be discussed between the two people. If these subjects are discussed and agreed upon, then the age difference should not be an issue.

I enjoyed the fact that four strangers can talk to each other openly about personal things. I think the four of us definitely had a connection. The more I got to know them, the more I opened up and laughed more, and this is not like me.

The waiter approached our table again and asked us if we needed more drinks as they were closing the bar. We decided to leave instead of buying any more drinks as it was 11.30. We paid and tipped the waiter, walked to our respective accommodation by torchlight, and said goodnight. Martina and

Matteo walked to their tents, while Anneliese and I walked to our rooms, talking more about relationship issues. As we reached my room, there was a table and chairs outside my room in a courtyard where we seated ourselves and talked a lot more. She opened up quite a bit, and she revealed that she had issues. Toward the end or our conversations, I felt like a life coach. I quite enjoyed the experience as it made me think of my life as I was offering suggestions to her. By then it was 1.00 am, and Anneliese needed to be up early for her game drive with Martina, along with some other people from another tour. We gave each other a hug goodnight. It had been a short day, travelling for three hours and 55 minutes, but it was a nice long evening.

I decided to sleep until 8.30 am. I wondered how Anneliese and Martina were feeling with very little sleep. I had breakfast with the rest of the group at the bus, and I asked Matteo how he was feeling after the late night.

"Not so well," he said. He went on to tell me the tale of his adventure that night. After he and Martina had left Anneliese and me, they walked to the pool for a swim. As they approached the swimming pool, Matteo noticed a security guard. They hid behind a wall that concealed the change rooms. When the guard moved to another location, Martina and Matteo snuck into the pool without being noticed. I assumed that Martina had an even later night than Anneliese. When Martina and Anneliese returned from their safari, they said it was good, but they were both very tired. After they had eaten, we all cleared and packed everything away, and went to our rooms to pack our bags.

Zimbabwe

We met the bus outside the Reception area, packed our luggage into the bus lockers, and left the lodge at 10.25 am. It was only a 30-minute drive to the Botswana–Zimbabwe border. We stopped at the Kazungula Border Post for Botswana departure formalities, but this did not take very long at all. From the border post it was only another five-minute drive to the Zimbabwe border, where we were delayed by queues of people who were also purchasing visas for Zimbabwe. An hour later, it was just a quick run into Victoria Falls, arriving at the Shearwater Activities Centre at 12.40 pm.

After we all disembarked the bus and walked inside the activities centre, Kondjeni parked the bus around the corner to avoid blocking the small street that was very busy with traffic and with pedestrians browsing the souvenir stores. Inside, we were greeted by the staff and asked to sit in the media room. Shortly after, they played a short clip on the screen, highlighting the activities we could book. White water rafting, cycling and helicopter flights were amongst the many activities on offer.

Matteo, Leon, and I booked a 22-minute helicopter ride. We were fortunate enough to be able to book a flight for that afternoon. Anneliese had already booked a flight through her travel agent in Germany, and her flight was scheduled for the next day. Martina decided not to book anything. It was a very long process for us to book the afternoon flight. The electronic payment system was not very reliable. I think the unreliability was a common occurrence as the staff possessed several card readers. When one reader did not accept a credit card, they would simply use another reader and repeat the payment process.

After one and a half hours, we had finally completed our transactions and walked to the bus where Kondjeni was waiting for us. He drove us to our accommodation, the Shearwater Village, a stunning resort with the usual bar, pool, lounge and restaurant. However, the resort we stayed in at Tsumeb, the Kupferquelle Resort, was far superior, with an Olympic-sized pool.

We were met by the t-shirt guy with the t-shirts we had ordered in Kasane. I was very disappointed with my purchase. My t-shirt colour was not the same as the sample I had picked, and it was too small. So, I think I will never wear it, and it will just become a souvenir.

Everyone received a welcome fruit juice on arrival. We were shown to our allocated rooms, which were in different parts of the resort.

I met Matteo at the bar and ordered some snacks and a couple of beers while we waited for Leon and for our transport to the Heli-base. I was disappointed with the local high-alcohol local beer, Castle, but the crocodile and chicken kebabs were delicious. Leon joined us, and shortly after, the driver for our transport arrived at 3.20 pm for a 3.30 flight.

On arriving at the Heli-base we were shown to the waiting area. It was a long wait but entertaining to watch the choppers take off and land back-to-back. After the long wait, we were asked to see one of the staff for check-in formalities. We were weighed one at a time and were given headphones with microphones and connection jacks. After another long wait, it was finally our turn.

As it was a rotary turnaround, people had to stoop low to board the chopper while the main rotor blades continued to rotate. Once on board, we plugged in our communication jacks and were able to speak to one another.

The view of Victoria Falls from the air was breathtaking. I have never seen anything more spectacular! The flight pattern was a figure eight to enable all passengers seated on both sides of the chopper to get perfect photo and video opportunities. Matteo and I spoke to each other during the flight through our headphones. This was very helpful, because he could tell me when he spotted something of interest on his side, and I could tell him when I spotted something on my side.

From the air, my imagination went to town. The falls themselves looked like water cascading into a crack in the earth: a mega earth-shattering crack! All around the main focal point of Victoria Falls, more cracks could be observed: cracks in the earth that we now call canyons, waterfalls and rapids. I imagine that when those cracks formed, it would have been life-changing for the animals of the region at the time.

View of Victoria Falls from the helicopter

As we were catching our breath from the aerial views, we started to land at the Heli-base and disembarked with full attention from paparazzi to entice us to buy photos of our flight. I purchased a USB stick with a record of the entire flight.

The five of us were ushered into a small room to watch an historic video of Dr Livingstone discovering Victoria Falls, along with our own trip edited into it. After the viewing, we broke up and started to browse souvenirs. I did not buy anything but went to the bar and bought three beers for us all. I found Leon, but we lost Matteo. His beer was getting warm, and the driver was getting impatient to take us back to the lodge.

We eventually found Matteo in a back room in the souvenir shops getting the flight video uploaded to his iPhone account. I handed him his warm beer and said, "We need to go, mate. The driver is waiting for us."

"Oh sorry, I just need a few more minutes."

Eventually, when everything was in place and uploaded, we were on our way back to the lodge. We arrived in plenty of time to have a beer at the bar and take a quick shower before meeting in the restaurant. I arrived first, followed by Anneliese, Martina and Kondjeni. The rest of the group joined us one by one, and we just ordered when we felt like it.

Our meal session was very pleasant, and the food was perfect. After the crockery and cutlery were taken away, a group of people appeared at the front of the restaurant dressed in loin cloths, started to beat out some music and commenced to dance. They were very good, and really got the restaurant up and clapping. They called on Martina and Anneliese to dance with them. The girls were very good and managed to mimic the high kicks of the dancers. They also beckoned for Matteo and Anesu to dance as well, and they were also able to get their high kicks up there.

Apparently, we were pre-booked to watch a play called "Simunye the Spirit of Africa," presented by the Victoria Falls Theatre. So, we had to leave the dancers and start our ten-minute walk to the theatre.

As I walked into the theatre, I looked around in awe as I descended the stairs to sit with Anneliese. It was a full stage, with full sound systems, and comfortable seats. Anneliese and I were seated at the front of the stage.

A very beautiful compere was suddenly on stage speaking to the audience about the play, the story behind the play, and the actors. As she walked behind the curtain, the stage suddenly came to life with performers and props. It was so impressive, but as usual with my weak bladder I needed to pee after having six or so beers!

When I returned, the play was in full swing and very impressive! It was the best play I had ever seen! And it was in Africa! The actors were so enthusiastic and athletic. I could hardly believe where I was, and what I was witnessing.

The whole story, the acting and the energetic dancing will be etched in my mind forever. I cannot think of any other word to describe it, apart from jaw-dropping.

As we were not allowed to use our cameras during the play, as a public gesture the cast performed a short routine after the main event to allow us to take videos and photos. After the short routine, the audience were allowed to walk up on stage to meet the cast and take more photos and videos.

After an exciting 20 minutes of talking to the performers and posing for photos and videos, our group slowly started leaving the theatre. The four of us (Martina, Anneliese, Matteo and I) walked back to the lodge by torchlight. We had another drink at the bar and again enjoyed each other's company. Anneliese and I had another long talk and agreed that the two of us had developed a connection.

Our last breakfast with everyone seemed disjointed. Some people would arrive when others had finished eating, or when someone was about to order. The whole breakfast experience was not as sad as I thought it was going to be. There were no speeches from anyone. That was surprising, as I thought Anesu and Kondjeni would have had a few parting words to say.

Eventually, we slowly started to leave the breakfast table, saying goodbye as we went. I think it was only Matteo who had a flight to catch that morning back to Switzerland. The rest of us were leaving the next day. I gave Anesu and Kondjeni big bear hugs and said goodbye.

We said goodbye to Matteo, and I promised to send his postcards to his friends in Switzerland. I thought it was quite nostalgic of him to send postcards to his friends, when he could have carried them himself and delivered them. I think it was all about having African stamps on the postcards.

I am not sure where everyone else decided to go, but it was just Martina, Anneliese and I left. We decided to just hang around locally and walk through the markets which were within walking distance from the lodge.

As we were leaving the Reception area to walk to the markets, there in front of us in the carpark were dozens of mongooses. They must have been very tame and comfortable with human activity to be this close. The previous place I had seen a mongoose was on the banks of the Chobe River in Kasane.

Our tour of the markets started out nice and quiet, but the further we ventured into the dozens of stalls, things started to get a little bit chaotic, with the vendors asking our names and where we were from. They really wanted us to buy something from their stalls and tried their hardest to talk us into buying. I had my mind set on an African throw. I had already bought my souvenirs along the way, and really, I did not even need another throw, but thought I would try to find one anyway. I found two stalls that sold them, but they were not quite what I was looking for. I had bought two throws in Solitaire, Namibia, and wanted to buy a few more the same, but the ones in the markets were not quite right. They were not really throws, but only pieces of material with African art painted on them. I thought they would be nice to have framed behind glass and hung on one of my walls at home. I eventually found a nice one at the markets and bought it for a friend in Australia.

Martina found some baskets and bought five of them in various sizes. We must have spent at least two hours walking around the markets, and after a while they all looked the same, as the stalls sold very similar merchandise.

We agreed that it was time to leave and have some lunch. We found a restaurant called Three Monkeys which was next door to the distillery. It was a nice restaurant on two levels. We sat at a table on the wooden deck and ordered some food. I refrained from ordering a beer for some reason. I am not sure why!

I think Anneliese and I ordered a light lunch of Bruschetta, and Martina ordered a chicken dish as she was hungry after her bout of stomach problems. It was a massive meal, and she was unable to finish it. She asked for a takeaway container to take with her.

When we left the restaurant, we noticed a young man standing on the street in a security uniform. It looked like he was guarding some parked motorbikes.

"He looks hungry," Martina said, as she walked across the street and handed him her box of left-over chicken. His beaming smile transformed his face from seriousness to happiness. Martina is a caring person, and I admire her for that.

We continued walking along the gravel street and noticed two men playing musical instruments. They looked like wooden xylophones, and their rhythm caught our attention. We watched them play for a while, and then Martina decided that she wanted to play. As Martina was being shown how to play, Anneliese also decided she wanted to play. They both played well under instruction, and the longer they played, the less instruction they needed. They were both very good! Above all, they were both smiling, and very happy!

The players and their instruments were set up outside a small shopping arcade. I left the girls to their music playing and decided to explore inside the arcade.

It was an interesting arcade. Perhaps arcade is not the right word to use, but it was full of shops selling wares that ranged from expensive art to fruit, other food and homewares. I bought a rather intriguing piece of material which I plan to frame one day. I almost bought a painting of African animals but refrained.

I reached the exit point, and found the girls were still playing the instruments and having a great time! I interrupted and showed them what I had bought. Then they wanted to go inside to see what there was to buy. After they thanked the players and tipped them, we went inside the arcade. They did not buy anything as they had already purchased at the markets.

We left the arcade and walked along the gravel road to reach our lodge and decided that we were going to chill in our rooms for a while. We discussed finding a nice restaurant for our last meal together, and I was delegated to do it.

As I was resting in my room searching the internet for a restaurant, I came across one that was quite close, and only $5 USD by taxi. The website looked very interesting, and I messaged Liam to ask if he wanted to join us. He eventually replied and said he would love to join us and asked for the address, which I sent to him as he was taking his own taxi.

I sat at the bar waiting for Martina and Anneliese and then realised I did not know how to get to the restaurant. I asked the bar tender if I could get a taxi to the restaurant, and he said he had a friend who could take us.

He called his friend to confirm. His friend wanted my WhatsApp number which was fine. I asked if he could pick us up at 5.30 pm.

Around 5.00, I received a message from an unknown number saying he was the taxi driver and was on his way to the lodge.

Martina and Anneliese met me at the bar, and I told them that I had booked a restaurant for the evening, and that I had also invited Liam. They were both very happy with my achievements!

At 5.30, I noticed a man walking into the bar. He started talking to the bar tender who directed him in our direction. I knew this must be the taxi driver.

"Is your name John?" he asked.

"Yes, it is. How are you?"

"I'm fine, sir. My name is Chris, and I am your taxi driver."

I introduced him to Anneliese and Martina, and we all left the bar, walking through Reception and into the carpark where his car was waiting. It was an old vehicle, and the passenger door did not open from the outside.

Once we were all inside the vehicle Chris said, "I have only started this taxi service. After, when my business is busy, I will buy a new car."

"I think your business will become very busy here in Victoria Falls, Chris," Martina replied.

"Thank you, miss. The look-out restaurant is about a ten-minute drive from here. Afterwards, when you are ready, you can call me, and I will pick you up."

I smiled and said, "I will do that, mate. Thanks."

After we arrived, we said goodbye to the taxi driver and started walking toward the main doors to the restaurant. We were all in awe of the beauty of this place: high cliffs in the background, and a view of the Zambezi River rapids running and snaking around the base of the cliffs. The cliffs were so close that it felt like we could reach out and touch them.

It was an absolutely stunning outdoor restaurant. The décor was contemporary with a modern twist. We were all extremely impressed, and Martina and Anneliese kept thanking me for choosing such a beautiful restaurant. It had close-up black and white photos of African tribal people and was decorated throughout in African style. It even had an art gallery, which I was interested in, but it was unfortunately closed for the evening.

We were shown to our table which was on the edge of the balcony, looking down at the river more than one hundred metres away. The three of us captured many photos of the landscape, and some group photos of the three of us.

Unfortunately, the sun had set early, and we were losing daylight fast. We wondered where Liam was because he would miss out on all these beautiful sights.

Just as we mentioned Liam, I spotted him entering the restaurant and talking to one of the waitresses. She walked with him to our table. We all greeted Liam, and we were happy to see him. He had been on a little journey to Zambia and back. He was wearing a nice African shirt that he had bought as a souvenir of his day's travels.

Liam is a good bloke, and funny. He had forgotten his reading glasses, and so he could not read the menu. He asked the waitress if anyone had left any reading glasses behind.

"I'll check, sir."

She came back to the table with three pairs of reading glasses that people had left behind. Liam chose one and commenced to read the menu. Only Liam would think of doing something like that.

We had a great night, with lots of laughs, and lots of drinks. Well, only I had lots of drinks, as Anneliese does not drink, Martina only drinks a little, and Liam had recently given up drinking. I ordered an Irish coffee to make up for all of them.

I decided to pay for everyone, for some reason – it must have been the Irish coffee – but when I tried to pay, all the machines were not taking my Wise card. It had happened previously at the Shearwater Activities Centre. One of the machines was bound to work, and they kept trying all of them until one of them accepted my card.

As we walked through the lounge toward the carpark, I saw our driver sitting in a lounge chair. He noticed us, smiled and waved.

"Are you ready to go?"

"Hi, Chris. Yes, we're ready to go."

Liam's driver was waiting in the carpark. We all said goodbye and entered our respective vehicles. I thought I would see Liam the next day, but I did not.

Chris drove us back to our lodge where we sat at the bar for a while. The three of us talked for quite a while, but then finally called it a night. We said our goodbyes and goodnights. Anneliese and I had a very long hug as we did not know if we would see each other the next day before I left for Johannesburg.

Martina left the bar walking to her section of the resort toward her room. Anneliese and I left together as our rooms were in the same direction.

"Maybe we could meet in the next life when things are not so complicated," I ventured.

"Yes."

As we walked closer to the point where we would separate to go to our own rooms, we both smiled and said, "C'est la vie!"

Johannesburg, South Africa

As my flight to Johannesburg did not leave until 2.15 pm, I had a relatively comfortable sleep-in until mid-morning. I walked to the restaurant for breakfast and found Leon sitting alone.

"May I sit with you?" I asked.

"Yes, of course."

We talked for a while before the waitress appeared. I gave her my order just as Martina joined us. As usual, we enjoyed each other's company over breakfast.

"I need to go now," I said. "I have to post Matteo's postcards to Switzerland for him, but first I need to return to my room to get the postcards. I'll see you a bit later before my flight."

While I was in my room, Anneliese messaged me saying that she had returned from her chopper ride and asking where I was. I replied that I was on my way back to Reception. When I arrived at Reception, I could not see her and started looking around. I saw her in the restaurant ordering breakfast. She was sitting alone and must have just missed Leon and Martina. I joined her and asked her how her flight was.

"It was so exciting! The falls are incredible." I noticed how excited she was telling me about the flight. "I have never been in a helicopter before. At first it was very scary, but once I looked at the falls, I forgot about my fears."

At that moment, Martina returned, walking through the restaurant. I waved to get her attention. She smiled and waved back, and joined us at our table. We discussed our plans for the day. I said that I needed to go to the post office, and they decided that they would walk to the Victoria Falls lookout.

After Anneliese had finished her breakfast, the three of us walked to the post office. It took such a long time to get served, and trying to explain that I wanted to send three postcards to Switzerland took even longer. I was grateful that Martina and Anneliese had waited for me before they went on their walk.

Once I placed the postcards into the post box, there was nothing else to do but to say goodbye with hugs and kisses. As we walked in opposite directions, I thought to myself, "I will miss Anneliese." Martina, too, of course, but Anneliese and I had developed a connection that must be mentioned. However, when we go back to our home countries and resume our normal lives, will that connection eventually dissipate?

I walked along the gravel road back to the lodge and was again pestered by people along the way asking me to buy their merchandise. They were part of the market with stalls set up on the main street.

I entered my room and checked my bags before carrying them to Reception to settle any outstanding bills. I decided to chill out in the lounge and wait for my transport to the airport, and to reflect on my whole trip, the people I had met, and the people I had classed as friends. During my chill-out session, Leon joined me as his flight was only two hours after mine. We just made friendly chit-chat. What else was there to say?

When my transport to the airport arrived at 11.20 am I boarded the minibus, and the driver spoke on the two-way radio to a dispatcher asking if there were any more passengers. The dispatcher said, "Yes, you have to wait to pick up Mr Matteo."

"Matteo left yesterday," I told him.

They did not know he had left the day before and wanted me to confirm that he had gone. I called Matteo on WhatsApp. Thankfully, he answered straight away. I had him on speaker phone and told him the predicament I was in.

"They won't leave the lodge until they have confirmation that you have actually left."

Matteo spoke to the driver saying, "Yes, I can confirm that I have left Africa, and I am now in Switzerland."

Suddenly, everyone was happy! I thanked Matteo and hung up. The driver then pulled away from the lodge on our way to the airport.

We arrived at the Victoria Falls airport at 12.00 pm. Check-in was a little confusing, but I succeeded in making it happen. Once I had passed through Immigration, I walked around looking at souvenirs, but I could not get in the mood for shopping. I missed Anneliese and the close friends I had made on the trip.

It was a feeling I had never encountered before. I was walking around the airport feeling a little lost. I had just lost the people I had spent three weeks on a bus with, and I had become close to some of them. It was a particularly low point of my journey. I did not feel like having a beer, or eating anything. I just wanted to be with my new friends.

As I continued to walk from shop to shop, thinking about Anneliese and the others, I noticed Leon sitting at the bar. I stopped to say hello and ordered a toasted sandwich and a beer. He told me about his next journey to Cape Town and beyond. I envy people like Leon. They can just go anywhere and not think anything of it: not think about what people think of them, not think about whether it will be a nice place, not think about the next day; just living and travelling for the day and making friends.

We said our goodbyes as my flight was being called. I left Victoria Falls on time at 2.15 pm and arrived in Johannesburg at 4.05. The South African Airways staff were very friendly, but unfortunately, they ran out of wine during the flight!

Immigration in Johannesburg was a bit of a trial, with long delays. Eventually, I managed to get through and found a porter to take my bag to the City Lodge for my overnight stay. The lodge was only a seven-minute walk from the airport along covered walkways.

I was at the pool bar by 6.20 pm, having a beer and feeling lonely, an unusual feeling for me. Nothing seemed real: the pool, the bar, the plane, the restaurant. However, I had a good meal and an Irish Coffee afterwards. I think I was in bed by 10.45.

As my flight to Hoedspruit was leaving at 10.30 am, I woke up early enough to have a good breakfast and checked out at 9.00. When I was exiting the elevator on the ground floor, I found about four porters waiting. I chose the one with the friendliest smile. He introduced himself and asked, "Which airline are you flying with, sir?"

"South African Airlines."

As we walked to the airport, he told me that it took him one hour every morning by bus to arrive at the airport for work. He went on to say that he enjoyed his work and meeting people.

We arrived at the check-in counters for South African Airlines, and I tried to tip him with Botswana pula, but he didn't accept the currency, and nor did he accept the Namibian dollar. I resorted to tipping him with 100 rand, which was the smallest denomination I had.

He smiled and thanked me as I proceeded to check in for my flight. After progressing through security, I found that I had plenty of time before boarding my flight. So I found a quiet café in which to sit and update my journal.

After my coconut water and espresso, I followed the signage to my departure gate, which was downstairs. All the passengers were herded onto a bus and made to wait for at least 20 minutes, which is a long time while standing with people within your personal space! We were packed in like sardines. We finally started moving and arrived at our aircraft, only to wait again before boarding the plane. They asked the elderly to board first. This was a bit of a problem as some of the elderly were on the other side of the bus and had to push through people to exit the bus.

One of the crew then announced something that none of us could understand. So we all started disembarking the bus, but we were not meant to disembark. One of the crew tried to tell us to get back on the bus, but we kept walking up the stairs and onto the plane. It was a bit disorganised, to say the least.

After that fiasco, we finally departed Johannesburg 30 minutes late for a short 35-minute flight, landing in Hoedspruit at 11.35.

After disembarkation, I found my "meet and greet" person from the Moditlo Lodge waiting for me at the baggage carousel. After I reclaimed my bag, he carried it for me to his car in the carpark.

It was only a 25-minute drive to the Moditlo Lodge, which was on the edge of Kruger National Park. I arrived at 12.35 pm and was greeted by two friendly staff with a welcome drink of fruit juice.

Checking in was quite unusual. The receptionist presented me with a nice wooden box which she opened in front of me. Its contents included three labelled envelopes: one for the safari guide, one for the safari spotter, and one for general staff. These were for tips at the end of my three-night stay. The box also contained a box of matches, and a pamphlet explaining optional activities that could be booked and paid for. A room key was also included in the box, along with information about the area and the animals that walk freely around the lodge. The information sheet emphasised that guests were not allowed to walk around outside the lodge or walk from the dining area to their bedrooms at night time, due to the animals around. We would be collected from our rooms and chaperoned to the dining area and back to our rooms by torchlight.

After the formalities were out of the way, a porter walked with me, carrying my bag to my room. It was an impressive sight: a wooden bridge over a dried-up river leading to a wooden boardwalk that took us to my room. We encountered a nyala and an impala outside my room, acting very tame.

A nyala outside my room at Moditlo Lodge

As I entered my room I was met by a large bathtub in the lounge. The room had a king-sized bed and separate bathroom and toilet, and was tastefully decorated with cushions, occasional chairs and wall art. The concertina glass doors opened fully onto the wooden veranda, giving uninterrupted views of the bush and some wildlife. I was impressed!

I was informed by the porter that lunch would be served at 2.00 pm and the afternoon safari would depart at 4.00. I took the time to settle in and explore my room before walking to the dining area. The tables were already set. There was a table for one person, which I assumed was for me, and then there were other tables set for two people, four people or six people. I ordered a beer and waited for everyone else to arrive as I had arrived 15 minutes early to explore the dining rooms, the bars and the pool.

People started arriving and sitting at their respective tables. It was a help-yourself lunch with a variety of dishes, ranging from salads to cooked meats, home-made relish, cheeses and desert. During our meal, I noticed a person walking around in the background with a sling shot. I do not know what he was using for ammunition, but he was there to scare off the monkeys during mealtimes. There were about three or four small monkeys hanging around waiting for an opportune time to jump up onto a table and steal some food.

When I had finished eating, I ordered another white wine. As I looked around at the other people sitting at their tables, I had a feeling of separation and loneliness. These were not the same calibre of people I had spent the last three and a half weeks with. They dressed differently, spoke differently, and acted differently. They wore what looked like expensive clothes and shoes. The women wore heavy make-up and jewellery. I concluded that I was going to need the free alcohol to be able to talk with these people, as they appeared to be of the upper class. As usual, I was the proverbial "spare prick at the wedding".

However, there was a young couple who seemed like "working class", as they were dressed in tee shirts and flip flops. They might have been upper class as well, but at least they did not dress to impress.

The dining area slowly emptied as everyone walked back to their rooms. I stayed for more wine, and by the time everyone returned, I had had four wines and two beers and was ready for the afternoon game drive at 4.00.

We meandered through the Reception area and out into the carpark where our open-top safari vehicle was waiting for us. We met our guide and spotter and went through introductions and preliminaries. The guide was the "meet and greet" person at the airport, and he called me by my name. This made me feel a bit special, as if I were a local compared with the other guests.

The safari vehicle was well set up. The spotter had a special seat on the bull bar with a powerful handheld spotlight. The guide had a good two-way radio. For the passengers, there were nine seats in total, with three rows of three seats. There was storage for a large Esky, and table and chairs. And of course, it was a Toyota Landcruiser.

I had no idea in what direction we set off in, but we appeared to be following a series of well-worn tracks. Again, I was not feeling as excited about the game drive as I had been when I was with my friends.

Our first encounter was a herd of wildebeest lying down in a dried-up area. After we moved on, there was a call over the two-way radio which I could not understand. The guide quickly turned down a narrow track and slowed down enough for us to encounter a hyaena all on its own. It was walking around at first, but then it sat down as we approached closer. This was an opportune time to take photos and videos.

Wildebeest near Moditlo

Once we had all taken enough photos, we continued on our drive. All the while, the tracker was taking note of the animal tracks in the dirt and informing us what type of animal tracks they were.

We rounded a corner that suddenly revealed a herd of giraffes feeding on tree branches. They were not quite as majestic as the giraffes in Namibia for some reason. Perhaps it was the colouring, or the fact that they seemed skinny.

We left them to continue eating their leaves while we drove toward a body of water to find two rhinoceroses, also eating vegetation, on the water's edge. They were black rhinos, and very large. They were very different from the ones in Etosha.

Two rhinoceroses near Moditlo

We concluded the afternoon's game drive with an afternoon snacks and drinks stop next to a pond. It was well-organised, complete with tablecloths, biltong, droewors, cheese and nuts, served with liqueurs, wine and beer. Before nightfall the guide and tracker packed up the tables and chairs and put the food and drinks away.

As we were driving back to the lodge, the guide suddenly stopped and pointed to a bush. We all looked at the bush, not seeing what he was seeing. He left the vehicle and walked to the bush and then came back to the vehicle to show us a small chameleon. It was very green, but as he handed the creature around for us all to hold, it changed colour. I had never seen anything like that before.

Upon arrival at the lodge, we were all greeted with liqueurs in the Reception area. We stayed long enough to sample the three different liqueurs. I noticed that nobody from the group spoke about the animal encounters during the afternoon. They were more interested in the liqueur shots and the souvenirs for sale.

We were chaperoned to our rooms by torchlight and given enough time (30 minutes) to shower and get ready for dinner. After that time, the chaperone would knock on people's doors to see if they were ready to walk back to the dining area.

Dinner was at 8.00 pm, and it happened to be a barbeque, or braai in South African. It wasn't just a braai; it was dancing and singing by the staff as they walked around the outdoor tree-covered braai area. It was a good show, and the chef spoke to us about the food and the traditional way that it had been cooked. We were then allowed to stand up from our tables and help ourselves to food. I was seated on my own with a family of four from Minnesota, USA.

The food was excellent, and during the meal, Terry from Minnesota expressed interest in my three and half week travels. I told them all about it: the desert, the animals, the bus, the sand dunes, the boat ride on the Chobe River, the border crossings, Victoria Falls, and the whole experience. He and his family were amazed by my travel stories and did not know that it was possible to see what I had seen. Their travel agent had sent them to this lodge direct from Minnesota so that they could see the animals. And that was exactly what they achieved, but without the travel experiences. I felt they did not plan their African trip very well.

After more food and more conversation, it was time to leave the braai area and go to one of the bars. As Terry enjoyed wine too, I suggested we grab a glass and walk up the observation tower to look at the stars. Terry and his wife seemed to like that idea, and we promptly took our glasses up the tower. I think their son and girlfriend went to their room.

Surprisingly for me, we enjoyed each other's company and the billions of stars above us. After we had finished our wine, we walked down the stairs of the tower by torchlight and walked to the bar for another glass of wine. We stayed in the bar and chatted a bit longer before they had to leave as they had an early departure the next morning. After we said our goodbyes, I ordered another wine to take back to my room and was chaperoned to my door. It had been a long day, beginning at Johannesburg, and then travelling to Hoedspruit and to the lodge, followed by a game drive. The day ended at midnight!

I decided not to do the morning game drives for my three-night stay to enable me to sleep in after my three and half weeks of waking up early, and my long days on the road. I slept in until 8.00 every morning and had breakfast at 8.30 when the morning game drive guests returned.

One morning after breakfast I spent the rest of the morning in or by the pool, swimming or writing. The water was a pleasant temperature, and it felt nice to relax after travelling every day.

On one of the days, a young woman entered the pool area while I was swimming. She removed her shirt and proceeded to enter the pool with me.

"Hello, my name is Mayra."

"Morning, I'm John."

She had an accent that I could not quite recognise. I assumed she was the partner of the other young person sitting with her at lunch the day before.

"Where have you travelled from, John?"

I told her about my three and half weeks of travelling and experiencing Africa on a tour. She was genuinely interested in my story and wanted to learn more. As we spoke, I was surprised at the level of the conversations we were having. She was very intelligent and intuitive.

"Are you and your partner travelling through Africa?"

"No, he is not my partner. We work together."

"What kind of work do you guys do?"

"We work for Teach for Cambodia. We recruit outstanding young university graduates and young professionals to commit as teachers in high-need schools, through the Teach for Cambodia fellowship."

"What a coincidence! My son is living and teaching English in Cambodia!"

"Maybe he would be interested in joining us. I will send you the website to forward to him, if you want."

We exchanged WhatsApp numbers and continued to swim and talk for quite a while longer before she decided she needed a nap.

"The early morning start for the game drive has made me tired," she said with a smile.

"No worries, Mayra, I'll catch up with you at lunch. Have a nice rest."

We said goodbye, and I continued to hang around the pool until just before 2.00 pm. I then decided to walk back to my room and get ready for lunch.

When I arrived at the dining area, my table was set for one person again, like the day before. A few people, including Mayra and her colleague, were already sitting at their tables waiting for the lunch courses to arrive.

When Mayra noticed I was sitting on my own, she gestured for me to join them at their table. I carried my drink and my journal to their table and sat down. Mayra made the introductions.

"John, this is Jose, my work colleague."

"Pleased to meet you, Jose."

"You too, John. Where are you from?"

"Cairns, in Australia."

"I have never been to Australia, but one day I will go."

Mayra said, "I also have not been to Australia."

"Where are you guys from?"

"We are from Peru," Mayra said.

"Wow! I would love to visit Peru one day."

Over lunch, we spoke at depth about our different countries: the best places to visit, the best food, the best time of year to visit. We also discussed the geography of our countries.

After lunch everyone dispersed except for me. I continued to sip wine and write some more. During one of my visits to the toilet, I noticed a bright-green snake on the ground. I did not think it was dangerous because we have harmless green tree snakes in Australia. However, when I showed the photo to one of the staff, he nearly freaked out. He said that it is a very dangerous snake in Africa.

At 4.00 pm, we were again ready at the Reception area to board our game drive vehicle. We reacquainted ourselves and boarded the game vehicle. Mayra sat next to me as her work colleague, Jose, did not want to come because he had too much work to do.

The first animals we saw were two rhinos by the water, and then a cheetah! It was one of the prize animals to see. The guide drove the vehicle closer to the cheetah through the tall grass, scraping along tree branches. We stopped within a comfortable distance and remained still and quiet while we all photographed and videoed the magnificent big cat.

Cheetah at Moditlo

We left the cheetah alone and attempted to find more animals, but they were a bit scarce that afternoon compared with the day before. However, we did find a nice place to set up our tables for drinks and afternoon snacks. We set up on slightly elevated, smoothly rounded rocks, overlooking the vastness of the flat land.

Again, we packed up just before nightfall. We drove in the direction of the lodge, with the tracker seated in his special seat on the bullbar, spotting for animals with his powerful spotlight. After some time, he spotted a lioness on the edge of the road. As we drove slowly closer, it leapt up and started walking in front of our vehicle for several metres before walking back into the bush toward a second lioness. We managed to take several videos and photos before they both disappeared further into the bush.

We continued driving back to the lodge without seeing any more animals. We arrived at 7.15 and were greeted with liqueur shots at Reception. We were then chaperoned to our rooms and back again to the dining tables. Dinner was at 8.00, and I joined Mayra and Jose to settle into a fine à la carte menu. The starter was a choice of either pea and mint soup with crispy bacon and sour cream, or yellowtail tuna tartar served with mango, capers and red onion. The main course was either grilled beef fillet or seared kinglip, or creamy mushroom risotto served with truffle oil and parmesan. Desert was crème brulé served with caramel popcorn.

After dinner I asked Mayra if she wanted to walk with me up the lookout tower to look at the stars. She said yes, but while walking to the tower she appeared to be a little worried about animals. I reassured her and continued to walk. We reached the tower and ascended the wooden staircase.

We sat in the comfortable deck chairs, gazing at billions of brilliant stars, all the while engaged in good conversation. We descended the stairs and left the tower to find our chaperone. He escorted Mayra first to her room while I stayed at the bar for another wine. When he returned, he then escorted me to my room.

I think I was in bed by 11.45. It had suddenly turned into a late night because dinner was not until 8.00, and by the time the food was ordered, presented and eaten, it was nearly 9:30.

The next morning most of the people left after breakfast, leaving just myself and a Brazilian couple who hardly spoke any English. Mayra and I had another engaging conversation before she needed to depart for the airport. She gave me a long hug and, to my surprise, so did Jose. We said our goodbyes, and as they drove off, I walked up the lookout tower to chill out with some music and look over the landscape until it was lunchtime.

During lunch, I was told that there would be no other people checking in on that day or the next. That meant that the Brazilian couple and I had the whole lodge to ourselves.

At lunch we were served lamb or fish and chips, with salads. It was presented and tasted better than it sounds.

Instead of having my usual quota of wine before the afternoon game drive, I walked back to my room and had a rest while I messaged Martina to see where she was on her journey.

She replied that she was in Johannesburg but that was not planned. I thought, "What a coincidence!". We agreed to meet for dinner when I arrived in Johannesburg. We planned to meet at 5.30 pm at a restaurant called the La Parada in Rosebank.

At 4.00 pm the Brazilian couple and I met in Reception, boarded our open-top vehicle and left the lodge for the final game drive. We travelled for quite a while before coming across four elephants eating trees. We left them alone and continued for a while before encountering a warthog. We rounded a corner to find a lion lying on the road. I got closer to this one than to the one in Etosha. He had a beautiful full mane and looked very regal.

Lion on the road near Moditlo

As it was starting to get dark, we drove away from the lion to find a place to set up the table and have some drinks. The Brazilian couple and I managed to speak with each other, but I think our sign language helped.

We packed everything up and drove back to the lodge. On the way we encountered a solitary lioness sitting on the edge of the track. It jumped up when we emerged and started walking in front of the vehicle until it strayed off into the bushes again.

We had our usual shots of liqueur on our return and were escorted to our rooms and collected after 30 minutes for dinner. Two tables were set by the pool, with some nice ambient lighting. I sat alone, and the Brazilians had their own table. Talk about awkward!

After I had eaten, I walked over to their table and asked if they would like to join me for a drink in the lounge. I gestured with the international hand signal of lifting my hand to my mouth pretending to drink something. They talked in rapid Brazilian and they both nodded.

I proceeded to walk to the lounge and sat in a comfortable seat having a wine. They appeared after about 20 minutes to join me, and ordered some drinks for themselves. We appeared to get along quite well. The husband spoke English well enough for me to understand, but the wife spoke no English at all. He explained to me that he learned English from watching American movies. I found that quite interesting.

After a few more drinks, we all said good night around 10.00 and were escorted to our rooms. I packed all I could to be ready for my departure the next morning.

It was nearly time for me to start my journey back to Johannesburg. In the morning, I sat in the dining area, and the weather was surprisingly cold. I had a jacket on and thought about going back to my room for a pair of jeans, but I had already packed them the night before.

I had breakfast with the Brazilian couple, again at separate tables. We did not communicate very much during breakfast. After eating, they said they were going to collect their bags from their room and would return.

When they returned, we made small chit-chat about how I must come to visit them in Brazil one day. Next thing, they were in an SUV, and they were gone. Suddenly, I was the only person in the entire lodge, apart from the staff. I stayed in the dining area to continue updating my journal until it was nearly time for me to leave. I walked back to room, threw some things in my bag and carried it back to Reception, along with my little wooden box. I had added some US dollars into the gratuity envelopes, and I hoped that they would be happy with my contributions. After the check-out routine, I said goodbye to the couple of staff who were with me, and they showed me to an SUV. I left Moditlo Lodge at 12.20 pm.

After arriving at Hoedspruit airport, I noticed a big line-up of people at the check-in counters. There were five check-in counters, and only two people serving. The line moved very slowly, but after some time another two people appeared to help with the check-in process.

I finally checked in and went inside for coffee and a look around the only two souvenir shops. We boarded the aircraft on time, departed on time at 2.30 pm and landed in Johannesburg at 3.25. The disembarkation and baggage collection process were so much easier than the last time I landed in Johannesburg.

I managed to find a baggage trolley and decided to walk myself to the City Lodge, the same place I had stayed the last time. The porter I had last time managed to wheel the loaded trolley onto the escalator. He made it look so easy that I thought I would try it. I approached the escalator and looked down at the moving stair treads. There were some people riding the escalator below me as I waited for the opportune time to wheel my trolley onto it. I chose my moment, and as I did the trolley started to fall forward and onto the people below. I had to use all my strength to pull the trolley up and lean it back toward me. So, there I was, balancing a full trolley and stooped behind it, looking very awkward. Thankfully, I made it to the bottom without crushing the people below. There is a definite art to this manoeuvre.

After checking in, I carried my bag to my room, which was upstairs and along a series of hallways and corners, eventually finding my room at the very end of a hallway. I entered the room, changed my clothes, and rushed back to Reception to organise transport to Rosebank. The receptionist made a phone call to the hotel shuttle bus and said it was going to cost about 600 rand. She went on to say, "An Uber will be much cheaper, sir." She showed me the app on her phone and the price. It was less than half the price of the hotel transport.

"Would you like me to order you an Uber?"

"Yes," I said. "I would like to go to the La Palma restaurant in Rosebank." After she made the booking, she gave me the car registration number.

"The car will meet you in the downstairs parking area in ten minutes."

She kindly summoned a porter who was standing next to the elevator doors and asked him to take me to the downstairs parking area. After waiting for more than 15 minutes, we went back upstairs to see the kind woman at Reception and explained that the car had not arrived. She checked her app to find that the car had gone to the wrong pick-up area.

"I think it would be better if you download the app yourself, as you will need it to come back to the hotel this evening," she suggested.

I downloaded the app, and she kindly showed me how to use it and where to be dropped off in Rosebank. Apparently, the La Palma restaurant was in a terraced mall, and the drop-off point for taxis is a short walk away.

My app said the Uber was on its way and would arrive in 12 minutes. I took note of the registration number. I thanked the receptionist immensely and complimented her on her kindness.

"Would you like the porter to go with you again?" she asked.

"No, thank you. I can find my own way now."

The elevator took me downstairs, and as the doors opened, there was a red car parked in a lay-by outside the carpark. There was a man with long dreadlocks sitting in the driver's seat, listening to some loud music. I checked the registration number, and it was my Uber. I got into the back seat, and we left the hotel. He had two phones: one holstered on the dashboard with the map screen up, and one that he was talking on as he drove. He would stop talking on the phone whenever we stopped at a traffic light and commence to text on the phone. When the lights turned green, he would continue to talk on the phone. A strange concept, I thought.

Johannesburg city was just that: a city. I did not know exactly where in the city I was, but I assumed I was not in the centre.

Our route took us through some housing suburbs. I was amazed at the houses. Every house had high concrete walls with razor wire installed at the top. Every house also had warning signs that security cameras were in use 24 hours a day. I must have seen at least seven security patrol cars as we travelled through the suburbs.

I then became a little uneasy and wondered about the authenticity of this Uber ride. I studied my driver and checked my surroundings. I checked the GPS map on my phone to compare it with the map on the driver's phone. Everything seemed to be fine.

We were further delayed due to traffic. It seems everyone was going to Rosebank for Friday night fun. I messaged Martina to say I would be about 30 minutes late.

I finally arrived at the taxi drop-off point in Rosebank, 45 minutes after leaving my hotel. I paid the driver and gave him the customary tip. I could see the terraced outdoor mall and walked toward it. I was mindful of my wallet and phone as I walked, after seeing all the protected homes through the suburbs.

I arrived at La Palma at 6.00 pm. I went straight to the bar and ordered a beer. It was already very busy. I read a message Martina had sent me, saying that she was waiting for me at the wrong place and that she would be about ten minutes.

I had ordered my second beer. As I drank, I turned to look outside through the doors I had entered. There were so many people wandering around looking through the windows of several shops and restaurants. Some people perused the many menus available. At that moment I recognised Martina walking in my direction. She waved and gave me a great big, beautiful smile.

As she entered the through doors, I placed my glass on the bar and walked toward her. We greeted each other with a nice long hug and walked back to the bar where I had left my glass. We ordered two more beers and shared our travel stories since we were last together with the group in Victoria Falls.

Martina is Spanish, and while her English is quite good, she has trouble understanding some English terms. We spoke about our small group within the Roaming Safaris tour and asked if either of us had heard from any of them. She had heard from Anneliese, while I had been in touch with Liam and Matteo.

We decided to video-call Anneliese in Germany, who answered almost straight away. She was ecstatic to see us and waved through her computer.

Unfortunately, we could only hear every other word she was saying as the restaurant was filling with people and becoming very noisy. We decided to say goodbye and that we would call back at a later time.

Martina and I decided to find a quiet restaurant and left the La Parada. There were so many restaurants and bars to choose from, all of which were busy. We eventually found a quieter restaurant called Proud Mary. As we entered the main door, the first things we noticed were the decor and the subtle aromatic smells. I turned to Martina.

"I think I like this place. Do you like it?"

"Si, I like it very much."

A waiter walked toward us and said, "Good evening, would you like a table for two?" We both nodded and eagerly said, "Yes, please." We followed the waiter to a nicely laid table for two.

When we were seated, we both looked around at our surroundings. We smiled at each other.

"It's nice, no?"

"It's very nice, Martina. It was a good choice to come here."

The waiter asked if we would like a drink to start with. We both ordered a beer each. We casually read our menus in between conversations while waiting for our beers. When the beers arrived, we still had not decided on our meal selections and asked for a few more minutes before ordering. The waiter was more than accommodating as he smiled and nodded as he left.

Martina asked, "You see something on the menu?"

"I think I'm going to have the steak. Have you seen anything you like?"

"I'm not too sure, but I think I like to have the lamb."

We drank half of our beers while talking, and then the waiter returned. We gave our food orders, along with an order of a bottle of red wine. To our surprise, he was back quickly with the bottle of wine and two glasses. He placed the glasses on the table and proceeded to open the bottle of wine. He poured a sample portion into my glass. I took the glass and sampled the taste. As usual with these tastings I said, "That's nice."

He smiled and continued to fill my glass, followed by Martina's glass. As the waiter left, Martina and I looked at each other and raised our glasses for a toast to our African tour, and to our friendship.

During the evening, our conversations revolved around travel, her past relationship, her father, her homelife in Spain, sex and spiritual topics.

Martina is an artist, and she showed me on her phone some of her recent work, which was very impressive. It was a series of drawings reflecting the past three and half weeks on tour with everyone, and her feelings for her father. It was very plain but with a splash of colour. I was quite impressed with her work. I think she does not know just how talented she is.

As we tried to continue our conversations, the noise of the crowd seemed to grow, and it was getting hard to hear each other, especially when Martina's English is hard to understand, and my Spanish is non-existent! We finished our bottle of wine and decided to leave. I managed to get the waiter's attention and asked for the bill which I paid for. We thanked him and tipped him generously. The waiter opened the door for us.

"Thank you, I hope you enjoyed your evening. See you again soon." We both acknowledged him with a smile, and I said, "We had a very enjoyable evening. Thank you."

As Martina and I walked to the taxi drop-off point, I was getting a different feeling. We walked closer to one another, brushing shoulders as we talked. She is very passionate about her homelife back in Spain and spoke a lot about her godchildren and her family.

We arrived at the taxi pick-up point, and we both ordered an Uber through our phones. While we were waiting, we hugged each other tightly and promised to stay in touch. At that moment, her Uber arrived. We kissed, smiled and said goodbye.

My Uber arrived shortly after, and I was back at my hotel around 10.00. This driver was completely opposite to the last driver I had. This one did not stop talking! At times I could not tell whether he was talking to me or to himself. It was an interesting 45-minute drive.

I took a glass of wine to my room, showered, packed for the next day and was in bed by 11.00. As I lay in bed watching TV, Martina messaged me, saying she had a great evening and sending me some affectionate emojis.

Leaving Africa

It was finally the sad day that I left Africa. I left my hotel with a porter carrying my bag to the check-in counter. It was a relatively seamless process, and once I was behind security, I embarked on last-minute airport souvenir shopping. I think I did well. Gifts for everyone under one roof!

I entered the South African Airways lounge while waiting to board my flight. I sat there for an hour and had the complementary snacks and drinks, but the lounge was very second-rate. I was very surprised about that.

I sat at the bar organising the new wallet I had just bought and updating my journal. I had a sense of sadness and loneliness because I was leaving Africa and the friends that I had made. At that moment I had a vision that all of us would meet again in the Namibian desert.

It was time to board, a process which is seamless when in business class. I left Johannesburg and Africa at 2.30 pm, bound for Singapore.

After take-off and during the meal service, I spoke with an air stewardess called Ivy. We seemed to have a bit in common, and she asked if I was all right and if there was anything I needed. I was busy updating my journal during the first part of the flight, and she asked if I was a writer.

"Yes, I am. I write in my journal every day, and I have written a book."

"What do you write about?"

"Everything and anything. I just like writing. The book I wrote is a fictional action and adventure book called *The Delta*. You can download a copy if you want." The more we talked, the more I thought we were establishing a connection. "Do you have WhatsApp?"

"Yes."

I gave her my WhatsApp number, not expecting anything.

During the first leg of the journey I did not sleep at all, really: 30 minutes here, 30 minutes there. The cabin was too warm, and I was actually sweating.

I arrived in Singapore at 6.40 am to find that my next leg to Cairns was delayed by 30 minutes. I messaged my son, Tom, to let him know as he was picking me up. I left Singapore for my final leg of the journey and arrived in Cairns at 5.30 pm. I had slept for maybe two hours on the flight.

I declared the biltong I bought in Johannesburg, hoping they would let me take it through, but they decided they would confiscate it.

Tom picked me up at 6:15 with some beers in his fridge for me for the one and a half hour road journey home to the Tablelands area. We arrived home at 7.40. I did not have any food for him, and so we managed to eat all the home-made biltong that had been in the fridge for a month. It was fine, and we stayed up for a while on the veranda, drinking and eating biltong. Tom left early the next morning to go back to Cairns for work.

This is the end of my story of an African experience I will never forget, and the friends I made that I will also never forget. For me, it was a life-changing experience that has changed me in small ways; I have deleted my Facebook account, my music genre has changed to soft contemporary music, I have not watched TV since I arrived home, and I do not even listen to commercial radio anymore. I feel more content with my life now, whereas before I was uneasy about my direction, not knowing which path to take.